MW01598878

Knowing the Unknowable

Gnosticism: Supernatural Spiritual Knowledge

Howard M. Snider, Ph.D

The Essence of Supernatural Spiritual Knowledge

Monistic Gnosticism Proclaims One Reality: Spirit

> These Gods are **Pure Spirit; Ultimate Unity**
> They **Created Nothing**
> They are, by self definition, the **True Gods** and **Good.**
> They decreed that Physical Creation is "**Flesh**" (Evil)

Dualistic Gnosticism (Creator God) Proclaims Two Realities: Spirit and Creation

> These Gods are **Pure Spirit**
> They **Created Time and the Physical Universe**
> They are, by self definition, the **True Gods** and **Good**
> They decreed that Physical Creation is **Good**

These two classes of Gods:

> Are vicious **Name Callers**
> They declare each other to be **False Gods** and **Evil**
> They are in contention and **War**
> They **recruit** humans to help them in this conflict.
> **Spiritualization** is the training phase

Human beings have confused these two Classes of Gods, in many aspects, and as a result have produced a **confusing** New Testament

Other Books by the Author

The Cultural Creation of Christianity
2005

Jesus or Christ
2007

Two Gospels
2011

Quotations and Questions crucial to the issues of this book

"For our sake he made him to be sin for us who knew no sin, so that in him we might become " (II Corinthians 5:21)

"It was to prove..."
(Romans 3:21-26)

Why did God need to prove that he was righteous; right?

"Right" about "What?"

Who needed this proof?

Why?

How was proof provided?

Who cares?

Acknowledgements

I am indebted to a vast number of people who, over the last sixty years, have been attentive and patient with my ruminations about topics relevant to Sociology of Religion and Theology disciplines.

The most gracious of these have been my family who have tolerated the thousands of hours of research and writing.

Many friends have read portions of this book in preliminary drafts. Their interest in the topic and comments, have been a constant help and encouragement.

I am indebted particularly to three friends who have influenced many aspects of this book.

Merrill Raber, a professional counselor whose work with people in the context of religious anxieties is related to topics of this book.

Wayne Wiens, a microbiologist whose side interest had been the discipline of socio-biology.

Dennis Koehn, a courageous social critic with many concerns about extreme "Christian" ideologies and their degenerative effects on individuals and society.

I will never forget the "Edmonton Group" who provided the social context for many creative thoughts relative to theological ideas fifty years ago.

Cover Design by Robert Regier

Table of Contents

Appendices

CHAPTER 1

Knowing the Unknowable

This book is about unknowable knowledge.

This book is about unknowable supernatural knowledge.

This book is about unknowable supernatural spiritual knowledge.

No human being has ever known anything about such matters? Human beings are natural beings, not spiritual beings in any supernatural sense. We have human spirits which are totally natural.[1] We are, by our very nature not supernatural spiritual beings. We are natural beings. By definition we do not know and cannot know anything about supernatural spiritual phenomena. We are made that way![2]

Regardless of the scientific truth of these introductory paragraphs, many, probably millions of human beings, claim to know about these unknowable things. They, in their thought system, have populated the unknowable supernatural spiritual world with spirits of various kinds: Gods, demons, angels, aeons, advocates, devils, christs, avatars, messengers and etc. etc.

They think they have such knowledge. They talk and write about such knowledge. For thousands of years many have written about their supernatural spiritual knowledge. Consequently we know what these people thought, what they think and what they believe. This book is about such human "knowledge" systems.

Many people claim to have a God with whom they interact and from whom they receive responses. They claim to know what these supernatural spiritual powers are doing in their supernatural world and what they have done and are doing in our world. They also claim to know what the Gods want them and everyone else to do.

How is this possible since human beings have no "supernatural spiritual knowledge?"

Why write a book about a topic of which I know nothing, absolutely nothing?

Consider the following observations.

I live in a society where multitudes of people claim to know many things about a supernatural world and the activities of "spirits" that dwell there. They form mental constructs of an imagined supernatural spiritual world. They actually believe in the reality of doctrines, ideas and ideologies about such matters. They develop a world view which is based on these mental constructs.

I hear these people talk and I read what they have written. But it is all contrary to the scientific knowledge which I value and believe. In this book I am grappling with the dogmas of "supernatural spiritual knowledge," which many people believe, and I am trying to describe and explain those dogmas in their own context.

Human beings who believe in "supernatural spiritual reality" engage in relationships with their fellow human beings in ways determined by their mental constructs of such matters. Cultural groups have their own God. They tend to fear, dislike and mistreat people who worship a different God. The data from the beginning of time provides incontrovertible evidence of this scientific reality.

The differences which people perceive are used to justify exclusion, hatred, exploitation and very often violence to the point of atrocities, war and genocide. The people who engage in such activities always claim to be acting according to the will of their Gods.

There are indeed exceptions to such observations. I would claim to be a member of such an exception.

Because I live in a "Christian society" this book is about Christian supernatural spiritual knowledge. Some natural human being in other societies should write a similar book about their culture and belief systems.

Most Christians claim to know what their God has in mind with plans of salvation, spiritualization and numerous other aspects of his relationships with human beings.

How do they know such things?

No human being actually knows. But there are many who think they have supernatural spiritual knowledge. They think they know what their God does and what he wants his devotees and every body else to do.

All these are Gnostics; "knowledge believers."

The English translation of the Greek word γνῶσις (gnosis) is "knowledge." Gnosticism, at least in its religious-philosophical context, is the body of knowledge which describes the perceived characteristics of the supernatural spiritual world and its activities related to human beings.

There have been many varieties of Gnosticism. In the western world there continue to be two dominant kinds.

One is called Monistic Gnosticism because the adherents believe (know) there is only one ultimate reality: spirit. The God of this kind of Gnosticism is known as the Monistic God or Ultimate Unity or Pure Spirit God or Transcendental Divine Unity and etc.

The other is called Dualistic Gnosticism because the adherents believe (know) there are two realities; spirit and physical creation. The God, in this case, is known as the Dualistic God or the Creator God.

These two kinds of Gods have been enemies since the beginning of time. The central point of contention is the question of the value of physical creation. The Monistic God has decreed that physical creation is "flesh." This is a condition of ignorance of supernatural spiritual knowledge. Such a condition is evil and produces corruption and degeneration.

The Dualistic God in direct confrontation with the Monistic God created the physical world, including his crowning creation, human beings, whose basic character is flesh. He, however, by decree declared all his creation to be good.

In the early decades of the Christian era the Creator God Gnosticism became dominant and condemned the Monistic God Gnosticism as heresy and persecuted its adherents almost to extinction.

Creator God Gnosticism became, by the fourth century, a significant part of the philosophical-religious and theological system of the documents which were finally incorporated into the New Testament. It became orthodox Christianity as we know it today.

The Bible is the principle reference and source for information about what Creator God Gnostics "know" about the supernatural world and the activity of its spirits.

Spirituality and its Proof

One of the central elements of contemporary Christian orthodoxy is the ideology of supernatural spirituality. This doctrine presupposes the existence of a spiritual world and the existence of specific kinds of spiritual beings.

A crucial aspect of this doctrine is the belief that under certain conditions, spirits from the supernatural world come to our world and do things here. Some people believe that these spirits reveal information to them about the activities of the Gods and their interaction with human beings.

Even in our scientific age, segments of orthodox Christianity believe that the Holy Spirit enters human beings and transforms them into spiritual beings even while they are still in this world. Such spiritualized human beings are then empowered to do physical miracles and even spiritual miracles!

Instances of such spiritual activities are central dynamics of the New Testament. A few examples are: walking on water; sudden healing of paralytics; turning water into wine; sudden calming of storms; restoring dead men to life and the transference of spiritual power by the laying on of hands.

In the New Testament it is alleged that this happened to Saul (Paul) of Tarsus, a number of his followers, the followers of Jesus of Nazareth and even Jesus himself. This was consistent with the belief systems of the complex of cultures in which Christianity developed.

Jesus and his followers, Paul and his followers were human beings. Scientific evidence indicates that human beings

6

cannot perform miracles. Neither can they access the supernatural world or acquire "knowledge" about that world.

Saul of Tarsus after the "Damascus Road vision" was convinced he could do these kinds of things.

Paul says nothing about Jesus of Nazareth but he does describe his "Jesus Christ" as "Son of God," "Lord" and other superlative terms indicating that he believed the "voice" of his Damascus road "vision" to be one of the most preeminent powerful Gods from the heavenly realms. This was his basic ideology as he preached and established churches in Asia Minor and Southern Europe.

Obviously Jesus of Nazareth is not Paul's "Jesus Christ" and has no relevance whatever to such a spiritual icon.

A few decades later, by the time other writers whose materials appear in the New Testament did their work such superlative terminology was common in the writings of the third and fourth generations of Christians.

Jesus of Nazareth, in his life time, was only a human being. His gospel was about the human spirit not about supernatural spirits.[3] But by the time the writers of the gospels of Mark and Matthew were working, Jesus had been transformed, by myth, into a supernatural spirit with the power to do miracles and control spirits of the supernatural world.

The gospel of Paul had decisively trumped the Gospel of Jesus of Nazareth in the theology of Christians by the end of the first century CE. It is that complex of myths by which many Christians still live in the 21st century.

What have been the consequences for the world in the past two millennia? What are the consequences for our society?

---

[1] See Appendix A
[2] See Chapter 8
[3] See Appendix A

CHAPTER 2

Confusing Elements in the New Testament

In three earlier books I attempted to unravel the confusions of the New Testament which had been caused by the cultural characteristics of three major thought systems at the turn of our era. Elements of those books are summarized briefly in a few following chapters and Appendices B and C.

In those books I attempted to review the formative cultures which influenced the world view of Saul (Paul) and his writings. He grew up in the Jewish Diaspora community in Tarsus and was a Roman citizen. He spent the major portion of his years of ministry in cities in Asia Minor. His world view was a coalescence of at least three cultures: Jewish, Greek and Roman; each of which was an amalgam of earlier civilizations. He was a man of the world in his day.

Saul while persecuting the "followers of Jesus" experienced a traumatic threat to his world view, resulting in a remarkable reformulation of the myths by which he lived. Central to this new perspective was a conviction that he had, in a vision encountered Jesus, who was for him now a supernatural spirit. A few years later he testified that he had received "spiritual knowledge" from this spirit.

Subsequently his mission to the world had two overpowering objectives. The first was the salvation of human beings from the consequences of their sin. This, in his gospel, is the "plan of salvation."

8

The other objective was the "spiritualization"[4] of those who had been "saved." This spiritualization of believers and their power to do miracles became something of an obsession for Paul and others who wrote the New Testament materials. To describe this phenomenon, I have coined the phrase: "plan of spiritualization."

As a result of this amalgam of Saul's conviction and ideas from many cultures and thought systems he produced letters addressed to some of the churches which he had established.

In the following two and a half centuries many other essays, theological tracts and documents related to Christian doctrine and church issues were written by a wide variety of authors. Some of these materials were similar to the doctrines promoted by Paul.

These variant documents were circulating through different geographical regions resulting in a confusion of doctrines, beliefs, rituals and behavioral patterns. Consequently the Christian church from its very beginning has been a fragmented patchwork of doctrines and practices resulting in feuding, even hostile, communities.

The same must be said of groups of people who claimed to be followers of Jesus of Nazareth. Jesus we must remember wrote nothing.

What we know about him may be summarized in a few sentences. He was born about 4 BCE. In his short life he became a social and religious activist, a threat to the social order of his society. For this activity he was crucified about 30 CE. In an historical sense this is all we know about the man Jesus of Nazareth. The rest is myth.

The books we know as the "gospels" were not written until the period 70-125 CE They are collections of stories which had developed in the oral cultures of the Near East during a period of forty to a hundred years after Jesus of Nazareth had been crucified. Other stories about Jesus were lost or hidden for hundreds of years.[5]

The fragmentation of the Christian church and the quarrels about doctrine and church practices which developed, even while Paul was doing his missionary work, expanded and became more intense after Paul moved to Rome. Although Christians constituted a miniscule proportion of the total population in the Roman Empire, their increasingly quarrelsome behavior about religious doctrines caused considerable social instability. As a result many Emperors in the second and third centuries CE persecuted them.

The Emperor Constantine, was more tolerant than most of his predecessors. In 313 CE he issued the Edict of Milan requiring toleration of Christianity. This failed to reduce the social instability. By 325 CE the Christians' fractious behavior forced him to deal with this problem. He organized a conference of bishops which met in the City of Niceae. (Nicene) He guaranteed safe passage to any Bishop who chose to attend.

An attempt to reduce confusion

Constantine, a pagan, was the keynote speaker at this Christian conclave and demanded that the bishops come to an agreement about their doctrines. With this in mind they spent several months in discussions and finally accomplished two things. They produced the Nicene Creed which encapsulated doctrines which became the "faith" of sizeable portions of the Christian church for almost two millennia. Secondly, from the hundreds of doctrinal tracts, gospels, letters and church polity statements available at the time, they selected 27 documents which they considered to be useful for catechetical instruction.

About forty years later, in 367 CE, Bishop Athenasius (in his 39th Easter Festal letter) mentioned this group of documents as being exclusively authoritative for the Church.

"These are the fountains of salvation that they who thirst may be satisfied with the living words which they contain. In these alone is proclaimed the doctrine of Godliness."[6]

These have been the "Holy Scriptures" of the Christian New Testament for eighteen hundred years. They are also sometimes referred to as the "Word of God."

Did the bishops achieve Christian unity with these definitive and exclusive documents?

Since that time there have been seventeen hundred years of confusion about what that collection of documents is actually saying. Contemporary Christianity, with its contradictory interpretations, antagonistic denominations and alienated sects, is abundant evidence of this confusion.

Other source material

We must remember there were hundreds of other books, documents, essays, gospels and letters available that were rejected by the religious authorities of that fourth century conclave. Many of these unselected materials essentially disappeared from the awareness of Christendom through most of two millennia.

A renewed interest in these materials occurred in the 19th and 20th centuries with the discovery of many early Christian texts found at Oxyrinchus, Nag Hammadi and other excavation sites of the Near East. Some of these parallel the gospels of the New Testament and some include previously unknown materials.

A few of these recently discovered materials are of interest such as: The Gospel of Thomas, The Gospel of Mary, The Gospel of Judas Iscariot and other "gospels" with names associated with followers of Jesus or the Apostolic Fathers Other texts claim to report events in the life of Jesus, events of his infancy, childhood, teenage years and adult life.

Many of these materials reflect variations of the doctrinal and miracle elements found in the New Testament. Some of these, particularly those purporting to be "sayings of Jesus," are consistent with the New Testament and in some cases are elaborations or condensations of the same or similar ideas. This has led some scholars to believe them to be authentic "Jesus sayings."

None of these materials predate the writings of Paul or the gospels in our New Testament. Consequently they have added little, if anything, to our understanding of Jesus of Nazareth. However they have added to our understanding of the variations in theological perceptions which appeared in early Christianity and the fragmenting problems which plagued the early church. They are useful in helping us understand the confusions so evident in the New Testament and the diverse types of Christianity through two millennia.

These materials and the materials in the New Testament are best understood if we recognize that the followers of Jesus of Nazareth and the followers of Paul of Tarsus have constructed different religions and therefore remarkably different ways of living. These differences have contributed in major ways to the confusions which plague modern Christianity.

Jesus and Paul: Two different religions

An awareness of these differences may help us unravel the contradictions and confusions we find in the New Testament.

Although the historical facts of Jesus of Nazareth are sparse, many inferences enable us to construct the humanity of this man. He seems to have been a story teller with considerable knowledge of popular Jewish wisdom stories, sensitivity to the social conditions of his society and a charismatic quality in his interaction with fellow human beings.

He was so recognized by those who followed him most closely during his lifetime. For them he was a social activist, teacher, preacher and mentor. He was a man who advocated and lived a life of positive loving relationships.

Those who followed his way of living found the human spiritual power to attain a quality of life which led to human spiritual maturity and the practice of constructive and redeeming human spirituality. These "followers of Jesus" had lived, practiced and taught his way of living to family and friends for a generation before Paul and his Gnostic Christianity appeared. Jesus developed a religion which emphasized a human "way of living."[7]

More than 20 years after the execution of Jesus of Nazareth, Saul of Tarsus, who had persecuted the followers of Jesus began establishing churches based on a "vision." It is of speculative interest to try to understand how and why he identified his mental construct, Jesus Christ, with the human being Jesus of Nazareth.

Paul's "Jesus Christ" construct had all the defining characteristics of the Greco-Roman-Hebrew Gods of the cultural complex in which Saul had lived. It was a religion in which the way of life was based on "ways of thinking." It was based on "belief" and "faith" in supernatural spiritual speculations rather than human relational ways of living.[8]

Jesus of Nazareth was not a Christian. He was executed more than a decade before Paul developed any of his doctrines which became Christianity. His early followers likewise were not Christians. They had learned and practiced a way of living which he had advocated and practiced.

In my earlier books I have called these people "Jesus Christians." A more accurate description would be simply "followers of Jesus."[9]

However some of the followers of Jesus, after his crucifixion, began to attribute to him characteristics of a hero as they understood this term in their Greco-Roman culture. Those who had been most influenced by this complex cultural mix and its philosophical, religious, and social practices came to understand their executed mentor in the context of the "spiritual knowledge" of these cultures.

In addition, some of these people, by the middle of the century, came under the influence of Paul's Gospel and his churches and gradually incorporated elements of that thought system into their world view. Such people might logically be described as "Jesus Christians."

We should not confuse "Jesus followers" and "Jesus Christians." They were significantly different. "Jesus followers" were committed to a way of living. "Jesus Christians" were committed to a way of thinking.

Polytheism and Plurality

Both Old and New testaments were written in polytheistic cultures. There were no monotheists. People worshipped their tribal, regional or occupational Gods. They were aware of their neighbors' Gods and sometimes found it convenient and beneficial to worship a number of Gods. In general each subculture considered their own Gods to be more pertinent to their needs if not also superior to other Gods.

14

The word God in the Bible, although grammatically a singular term, refers to individual Gods and often to a whole class of spirits. For example, the Elohim (the God of the Creation account) was a plurality. Thus the Creator God was a class of Gods not a monotheistic God. In this book the words "God" and "Gods" are interchangeable.

In addition to these confusing factors there was another religious-philosophical world view common among intellectuals in the centuries surrounding the beginning of our era. This world view was a complex of versions, dealing with the experience of spirituality, particularly "knowledge of supernatural spirituality" which has its origin in "beliefs" about the activity of the Gods. This spiritual knowledge is hidden from human beings until they experience a relationship with the supernatural spiritual world. These variables are the principal interest in this book.

Scholars ordinarily refer to these matters in a term which arises from the Greek word "gnosis," which in its English translation is "knowledge." When used in a religious context it refers to a special kind of knowledge. Gnosticism refers to esoteric supernatural spiritual knowledge.

---

[4] See Glossary for definition of this word
[5] Grun, Bernard – The Timetable of History, Page 26 This source dates the earliest gospel a few years earlier than the Timeline in Chapter 3.
[6] www.ccel.org/ccel/schaff/npnf.xxv.iii.iii.xxv.htlm #6
[7] Appendix A
[8] see Jesus or Paul 2007
[9] See Appendix B

CHAPTER 3

New Testament Time Line

In addition to all the complexity indicated in the two introductory chapters there is also confusion about the 27 documents in the New Testament. It is often assumed they were written by the men whose names appear on the documents. It is sometimes assumed they were written in a successive time sequence from Matthew to Revelation. Both assumptions are in serious error. A time line indicating date of writing and authorship follows. It is crucial to an understanding of the New Testament.

The historical evidence of "events" reported in the New Testament is sparse. There are references to Roman authorities where dates are known. The historian Josephus reports the crucifixion of Jesus of Nazareth; an event dated about 30-31 CE.

Scholars, in an attempt to provide some clarity about events mentioned in the New Testament have used a number of inferential approaches. References to Roman political and military variables have been the most useful.[10]

The vocabulary, grammar, writing style and particularly the subject matter and problems dealt with, since they are author and time bound are also useful.

The sequence of dependency is another major factor, particularly in a culture where the development and transmission of literature is oral. Some materials reflect elements of earlier materials, oral or written, and therefore must have been written later.

16

For two thousand years most Christians have believed that Paul, the founder of the Christian religion in the sixth and seventh decades CE wrote 13 of the 27 documents which appear in the New Testament. In recent years this assumption has been challenged by scholars who have paid serious attention to the variables indicated above.

Many of these scholars have concluded that six of the documents attributed to the apostle Paul were written by other writers who used the name Paul. From this perspective there were three different writers all claiming to be Paul. The Apostle Paul (Saul of Tarsus) sometimes called the authentic Paul is the Radical Paul in the time line. The other two Pauls are known as pseudonymous Pauls (false Pauls) and are called conservative Paul and reactionary Paul.

The following New Testament Time Line, representing these perspectives, was constructed by Borg and Crossan of the "Jesus Seminar" (recently renamed "Westar."). I have added the approximate data relative to the Roman emperors.

The birth dates of Jesus of Nazareth, Saul of Tarsus, the crucifixion of Jesus and the conversion of Saul are important dates in the early years of the Time Line. The authorship and approximate dates of many of the New Testament documents are indicated in the Time Line.

---

[10] Grun, Bernard – The Timetables of History, Pages 26-28

New Testament Time line [1]

Augustus-Tiberias-Caligula Claudius	Nero	Vespasian Titus Domitian Trajan	Hadrian
4bc 10ce 31 43	55 65 75	90 95 100	135+ [2]

```
*---Jesus----*
         ^
     *--Saul------conversion---Radical Paul*    *Conservative Paul*    *   *Luke*   *Reactionary Paul*
```

Radical Paul	Conservative Paul	Luke	Reactionary Paul
Romans	Ephesians	Luke	I&II Timothy
I&II Corinthians	Colossians	Acts	Titus

---

[1] Borg and Crossan – Time Line. The approximate dates of Roman emperors have been added
[2] Approximate dates

CHAPTER 4

The Context of First Century Literature

Jesus of Nazareth was a human being not a supernatural being. He talked about and practiced a way of living that expressed a loving human spirit. This way of living called into question the religious and political way of life based on supernatural allegiances and a rigid social stratification structure on earth. For this he was crucified.

Since he was a human being he could do no miracles. It was not until the writings of Mark and Matthew appeared in the early 70s of the first century CE were there any written miracle stories about Jesus. The stories about Jesus' activities, including the performance of miracles are myths. But they are dynamic life changing myths for many people.

Six bodies of evidence support these contentions: The social context, the nature of oral societies, the ethos of authorship, the testimony of the authentic Paul, the essence of myth and the evolution of ideas.

The social context

Anyone who produces written material lives in a social context and responds to events and ideas encountered in that context. What they write is colored by the complex of their experiences. If we are to understand any written material we must understand the social context which produced it.

There is a general understanding that we should know the language in which the New Testament was written and the processes of translation. But very few people know what the complex of cultures was 2,000 years ago. They do not know the elements of the world views and the myths that gave meaning to the people whose writings they are reading.

The social context of the first century CE was a culture in which supernatural powers were everywhere present and active. These powers essentially controlled all aspects of human existence, especially for the masses of people who were poor and powerless.

The New Testament is often read in the social context of the 21st century. This results in vast distortions, misunderstandings, confusion and frequent intellectual and psychological trauma.

The nature of oral societies

The Greco-Roman world consisted of many non-literate societies. Literacy rates were 10% or less, consequently they were largely oral societies. In such societies people told stories about their understanding of events and ideas that affected them.

Some of those who followed Jesus during his life time were distraught and confused after his crucifixion. For them he had been a remarkable teacher and caring loving person who helped them to understand the social consequences of their stratified society. He had made them aware that such social differentiation was destructive for all human beings, especially the poor. He taught them that such a way of living was contrary to his God's intention for human beings. His God desired a society where all human beings were equal.

These followers of Jesus lived in a society where almost everyone believed that the supernatural world of the Gods, demigods and all kinds of other spiritual powers intruded into this world and even entered into human beings and did mysterious and heroic things such as miracles. Such ideas were a crucial part of their world view.

What was the nature of their discussion as they recalled their time of companionship with their mentor? What kind of memories did they have? What kinds of stories did they tell to their neighbors, friends and other acquaintances? These acquaintances repeated what they heard to their acquaintances.

Oral stories can go through many retellings in a short time. Each retelling is known, in the social sciences, as a generation of the story. How many generations of these stories would there be in a week, a year, a decade or forty years?

And each generation of the story has two phases. When a story is told certain elements grab the hearer's attention. These hearers are always selective. They tend to hear and remember certain aspects of the stories. In addition, their repetition of the story is a modified story as they incorporate elements of their own world view. Oral stories, after they pass through even a few generations, are inevitably major modifications of the original story.

In a short time, even a decade or so, such modified stories become understood as social truths (myths). Such stories were the resource materials used by the writers of the New Testament.

The ethos of authorship

There were no copyright laws in the early centuries of our era. Authorship of that period is uncertain.

Writers hope their materials will be read. A powerful device to attract attention to the writings of an unknown author is the use of the name of a hero or people who have been important in their cultural past. Such names carry social power long after the people have died. Names like Matthew, Mark and John carried considerable social power through many decades and even centuries. They are still quoted in support of doctrinal commitments to this day.

Authors of the 21st century are burdened with the necessity to reference the sources of ideas, or even a sentence or phrase which is not their own. No such anxiety troubled authors in the Middle East two thousand years ago. People told stories, changed them at their whim and embellished them for their own purposes.

Any reader of that era took these realities into account and probably found their life enriched by such liberalities.

The testimony of the authentic Paul

The radical Paul (sometimes referred to as "authentic Paul") wrote letters to seven or more of the churches which he had founded in Asia Minor and South East Europe. In these he attempted to reinforce the theological dogma of his supernatural commission, and dealt with church problems.

In the context of convincing church members that he was a "true disciple" and declaring himself to be a superior disciple he points to miracles as the surest proof.

> "The signs of a true disciple were performed among you in all patience, with signs and wonders and mighty works." (II Corinthians. 12: 12)

Paul claimed that his Jesus Christ" was a supernatural being, even a "Son of God" and therefore, certainly a supreme representative of the supernatural spiritual world.

The most significant evidence that Paul could have presented, to prove that Jesus was sent from God, was to report the miracles which he did. However he does not report a single miracle performed by Jesus of Nazareth. Why?

There are a few probable answers.

* He had no knowledge of any miracles! A very weak argument since he had intimate and prolonged contact with Jesus' followers whom he had persecuted.

* He thought that miracles were irrelevant to his gospel. This is even a weaker argument since proof of the divinity of Jesus was the cornerstone of his gospel.

* Jesus did no miracles. This must be true. Paul provided the incontrovertible evidence! He reported nothing about miracles performed by Jesus.

But the Gospels describe miracles that Jesus did. Where did these stories come from?

From a scientific perspective miracle stories evolved through generations of story telling in oral societies.

The essence of myth

Does the word "myth" require explanation?

Myth is not fiction. It is not fairy tale. It is not history. It is neither true nor false.

It is a story or a complex of stories by which people live. All human beings, without exception, have stories by which they live. All people believe their myths to be significant and, for them, true! A myth is the statement of the world view of an individual or homogeneous community.

Myths answer the ultimate questions and thus become explanations for all that is, including the unknown and the unknowable. They make life meaningful. They are crucial to individual and societal identity.

The evolution of ideas

There is no absolute consistency from author to author in the New Testament materials. But it is also true that individual authors change their perspective on many issues, even in a short time. We should expect the "radical Paul" to modify his theological ideas from time to time. He wrote at least seven letters over a period of a number of years. They, in several ways, demonstrate this human reality.

In my fifty years of writing about sociological and theological topics my understandings have changed. The distinctions I found between the gospel of Jesus of Nazareth and the gospel of Paul of Tarsus have expanded.

In earlier books I have used "Jesus followers," "Jesus Christianity," and "Jesus way of living" interchangeably.

Now, after thinking about this for some years, it seems that "Jesus way of living" is the better description of Jesus of Nazareth while he was alive, and also a better characterization of the gospel which he proclaimed.

After his crucifixion "Jesus followers" is appropriate for those who remained true to his way of living.

Jesus was not a Christian. Christianity did not develop until Paul established churches more than a generation after Jesus was crucified. By that time some "Jesus followers," particularly those who lived in Jewish Diaspora communities where Paul's gospel was popular, were influenced by elements of that myth.

At the same time Greek associates of the Diaspora synagogues were attracted to the developing myths about Jesus of Nazareth, particularly the ethical dimensions.

Both of these groups joined in the creation of a world view which incorporated a radically modified version of the Jesus myth which had transformed him into a Greek Christ consistent with Paul's theology. This system of thought might logically be called "Jesus Christianity."

But this was a two-way social interaction. Some elements, particularly ethical elements, of the gospel of Jesus of Nazareth had been incorporated into their thought system. The writings of the pseudonymous Pauls and the gospels of the New Testament reflect ethical teachings of Jesus of Nazareth. The word "love" is the most prominent example. [11]

In spite of these common ethical considerations the crucial difference between the gospel of Jesus and the gospel of Paul remains.

---

[11] Galatians 5:22

CHAPTER 5

The Gnostic Source of Paul's Gospel

Paul in the promotion of his gospel argued that Jesus of Nazareth, who had been crucified almost twenty years before he began his ministry, was a "Christ" from the supernatural world.

In his seven letters to the churches he makes no mention of the Damascus road "vision." He makes no reference to supernatural incidents associated with his change of mind about Jesus of Nazareth. Neither does he report anything about supernatural cosmic events attending the birth of Jesus of Nazareth. The same is true about the circumstances surrounding the crucifixion and the resurrection.

We have to wait a generation before we learn about those stories from Mark and Matthew or even longer; the end of the century, when Luke embellishes the oral stories which had been developing in the preceding 65 years.

Christmas, Easter, and the Damascus Road Vision are the most crucial myths in Christianity. But, Paul says nothing about these events in his letters which elaborate his gospel. These dramatic events are apparently insignificant for Paul, or never occurred! Myths take time to develop!

And even more astounding, Paul seems to know nothing of the life and ministry of Jesus of Nazareth; not even miracle stories.

From all of this we must conclude that the "Jesus" whom Paul talked about throughout his ministry and writings, is not Jesus of Nazareth, but an entirely different Jesus.

Paul's Jesus is a spirit; a messenger, an advocate, a Christ from the supernatural world. He had concluded, in his Arabian Desert retreat, that Jesus of Nazareth had been resurrected and was now a supernatural spirit. This doctrine is consistent with the mythology of Greco-Roman culture which was a significant part of his childhood and teenage years. It was also consistent with Gnostic thought of his time.

However Saul of Tarsus, in his mature years, knew about the followers of Jesus and his crucifixion.

He persecuted these followers. While on the way to Damascus to pursue this mission, some intense, traumatic, emotional experience demolished his world view. This experience initiated the three-year retreat in the Arabian Desert and Damascus during which he created a new world view. This was an agonizing experience as any human being knows who has found a controlling world view inadequate and then had the courage to structure a new world view - a new myth by which to live.

The sources of Paul's gospel

During this time of spiritual retreat he formulated his gospel which he later preached and by which he established churches. He did this without the help of the people who had been the closest associates of Jesus of Nazareth; the disciples and followers whom he had been persecuting.

He depended entirely on supernatural help, a revelation.

"...The gospel which was preached by me is not man's gospel. For I did not receive it from man nor was I taught it, but it came through a revelation of Jesus Christ." (Galatians 1:11-12)

The essence of this gospel was a particular interpretation of the crucifixion which was according to the will of God.

"Grace to you and peace from God the Father and our Lord Jesus Christ, who gave himself for our sins to deliver us from the present evil age, according to the will of God" (Galatians 1:3-5).

Paul's gospel did not originate with Jesus of Nazareth, his disciples, or any of the followers of Jesus. All of it came from his conviction that a supernatural spirit had talked to him, especially to him, and given him a message and a commission. He had experienced a spiritual birth initiated by a supernatural emissary, Jesus Christ.

And this was only the first of many more supernatural visitations.

"Christ is speaking in me." (II Corinthians. 13:3)

For about two decades after the Arabian Desert reconstruction of his world view, he preached his gospel and established churches. This he did in spite of failures and the defection of early believers.

"For the word of the cross is folly to those who are perishing, but to us who are being saved it is the power of God." (I Corinthians. 1:18)

The cross, the key event in the whole drama of the plan of salvation, is the power of God. It is enough, according to

Paul to save believers from the wrath of God. They would not suffer the normal consequences of their sin.

Paul, throughout his life had to deal with his own sense of sin and its possible consequences. In doing this he was responding to the universal problem of all human beings.

But he also had to deal with a major theological dilemma. His Creator God had created human beings as flesh (the condition of spiritual ignorance) with the potential, even a tendency, to disobey, in either case, a condition of original sin. Human beings are both evil and sinful.

Saul had two profound ultimate problems related to sin. One was God's implication in the sin problem. The other was the consequential problems for human beings. Paul had explanations for both.

God's involvement in the sin problem is the subject in later chapters. The human problem with the consequences of sin engages the attention of the plan of salvation in the next chapter.

CHAPTER 6

The Plan of Salvation

Human beings had been made by the Elohim (Creator Gods).
They disobeyed his commands. Consequently they were evil
and their Creator God decreed that they would die. The
consequences of sin are terrible.

> "… sin came into the world through one man…so death
> spread to all men." (Romans 5:12) "The judgment
> following one trespass brought condemnation."
> (Romans 5:16b)

Paul promoted these Gnostic supernatural principles. They
were the prerequisites for his gospel.

Human beings in all cultures developed sacrificial systems in
an effort to pacify their Gods with the hope of reducing or
eliminating punishment. But the Creator God found such
sacrifices inadequate. The creator God finally did it right.
He, according to Gnostic thought, sent his Son to earth to be
an adequate sacrifice to undo the consequences of evil and
sin.

This scenario is known by Christians as the plan of salvation.
It was a mysterious secret from the timeless time before the
world began. But in the first century CE, Paul of Tarsus was
entrusted with knowledge of this plan and its purpose.

Matthew

The Book of Matthew was written in the eight decade CE.
By this time oral stories had developed details of both the
birth and death of Jesus of Nazareth.

"…do not fear to take Mary your wife, for that which is conceived in her is of the Holy Ghost; she will bear a son and you will call his name Jesus, for he will save his people from their sins.(Matthew 1:20b-21a)

In Matthew's account there were wise men from the east and a moving star. Similar events had occurred at the birth of Mithra, two thousand years earlier.

Luke

Luke wrote in the last decade of the first century CE. By that time a collection of stories, coupled with the plan of salvation doctrines had become the crucial world view of Luke and other Christians. It was a life controlling set of myths.

He reports the end of the century stories of Saul's conversion and several sequential events that marvelously embellished whatever had precipitated Saul's change of mind about Jesus of Nazareth sixty years earlier.

"Now as he journeyed he approached Damascus, and suddenly a light from heaven flashed about him. And he fell to the ground and heard a voice saying to him, 'Saul, Saul, why do you persecute me?' And he said, 'who are you, Lord?' And he said 'I am Jesus, whom you are persecuting.'" (Acts 9:3-5)[12]

Luke continues the story which reported that Saul, now blind, and his companions proceeded to Damascus where a remarkable event occurred.

"So Ananias departed and entered the house. And laying his hands on him said, 'Brother Saul, the Lord Jesus, who appeared to you on the road by which you came, has sent me that you may regain your sight and be filled with the Holy Spirit.'" (Acts:9:17)

Who was this Ananias? Was he, perchance a Diaspora Jew or a Greek friend of the synagogue in Damascus and something of a follower of Jesus? He had a vision, a message from the Lord of the supernatural world, and received an order. He was about to perform two miracles: the restoration of Saul's sight (esoteric enlightenment?); and the endowment of Saul with the Holy Spirit.

All of this before Saul had his spiritual retreat in the Arabian Desert. All this before Saul had reformulated his world view or formulated his Gospel.

Ananias knew nothing of Paul's gospel since it didn't exist. He had no knowledge of how to be saved and be a Christian! Yet he recognized Saul as a brother. What kind of a brother? Was he just a fellow Jew? He seems to have access to elements of supernatural knowledge and its miraculous power. He had crucial Gnostic characteristics!

Luke, by the end of the century, had become a radical apologist for Paul's exclusive gospel.

> "Neither is there salvation in any other: for there is none other name under heaven given among men, whereby we must be saved." (Acts 4:12 KJV)

John, some decades later, has his own version of the gospel and is equally convinced of its exclusive character.

> "He who believes in him is not condemned; but he who does not believe is condemned already, because he has not believed in the name of the only son of God." (John 3:18)

Christians for two millennia have been acquainted with John's version of the plan of salvation, and the common assumptions of its purpose. The most common scriptural support was written a century after the crucifixion had occurred.

> "For God so loved the world that he gave his only Son, that whoever believes in him should not perish but have everlasting life. (John 3:16)

By the second century John was promoting this modified and developed version of Paul's Gospel and was inviting people to respond and join the Christian Church. He pointed to three attractive motivations: the love of God, the fear of perishing and everlasting life.
Paul a century earlier had written a summary of his gospel.

> "Grace to you and peace from God the Father and our Lord Jesus Christ, who gave him self for our sins to deliver us from the present evil age, according to the will of God." Galatians 1:3-5)

In Paul's version it is not God but Jesus Christ who gave himself for our sins. There is no mention of God's love or about perishing. Paul mentions nothing about eternal life.

In the cultures of the Near East, at the time the New Testament was written there were no Gods, except the Monistic God and his female minion Sophia who loved human beings. [13] Other Gods, including the Creator Gods interacted with human beings only in manipulative ways for their own interests. All human beings lived in fear (terror) of the Gods, particularly their own tribal and cultural Gods. And their terror was justified. The Gods, if they were displeased in any way, punished their devotees.[14]

John's version was a human oriented gospel. He promoted this Monistic Gnostic element of a loving God; a God who provided a way to escape from perishing and a God who promised everlasting life. Would any human being reject such options?

But John was in large measure a Creator God Gnostic. In his gospel there were conditions! Human beings had to believe in the efficacy of the dramatic acts in which God's Son (Paul's Jesus Christ) was the principle actor.

The plan of salvation is grounded in the crucial aspects of sacrificial systems. Every one in Greco-Roman-Hebrew culture was acquainted with sacrificial rituals and their purposes. All of this made good sense in the world in which they lived.

A summary of the plan of salvation

This Plan may be viewed as a Drama with six acts; all of them supported by John.

1) The entire human race is sinful and doomed to death and some kind of punishment.
2) A perfect sacrifice would pacify their Creator God and He would not hold their sins against them.
3) The only adequate sacrifice was the Son of God. Either the creator God gave his son or Jesus Christ gave himself as the sacrifice.
4) This Sacrifice effectively assuaged the wrath of God.
5) Human beings who believe this scenario will be saved from the consequences of their sin-eternal punishment.
6) Some believers will ultimately be resurrected as spiritual beings and spend eternity with the Creator God and his Son in Heaven.

All of this is based on the assumption that the Creator God is a God who loves human beings in some conditional way. This conditional doctrine with it Monistic Gnostic undertones is a remarkable myth developed over hundred year span.

A human-oriented plan based on a loving God

Human beings in general are selfish. They began to think that the Creator Gods cared about them. Therefore what they hear from God are words that support this viewpoint.

"… Come to me all who labor and are heavy laden and I will give you rest. Take my yoke upon you, and learn from me; for I am gentle and lowly in heart, and you will find rest for your souls. For my yoke is easy and my burden is light." (Matthew 11: 28-30.)

Is this the Creator God who expelled Adam and Eve from the Garden and condemned them to death and punishment? Is this the Creator God who swore wrath against his human beings for multiple ages of time.

"I swore in my wrath, they shall never enter my rest." (Hebrews 4:3)

What do the Gods think about this human interpretation of the crucifixion?

We must remember some facts about the spirit world. According to Gnostic dogma supernatural spirits do not sin. In their own perspectives they cannot sin. Sin is exclusively a problem of human beings. The Gods do what they do, and what they do is right (just) even though it is arbitrary, whimsical and generally disastrous for human beings. Who dares question the Gods?[15]

The Gods, all Gods, have always acted solely in their own interests. They have manipulated human beings for their own purposes. Has the Creator God now, in the first century CE, had a conversion, or is this particular doctrine of love another manipulative device designed to further their objectives in the great supernatural spiritual conflict?

Was the Creator God different than other Gods?

According to Gnostic thought the Creator Gods had designed the plan of salvation before the world began. Is it possible they had additional plans relevant to the supernatural spiritual world and their own interests which required this love dimension?

Is it possible that saving human beings from the consequences of sin was only a preliminary event? Is it possible that its success was the prerequisite to much more significant cosmic events which also had been planned before the worlds began! Human beings, in general, can only speculate about such things. But Gnostics know!

Paul drops many hints in his letters which suggest that he knew much about the purposes of these plans and was deeply involved with their realities.

The Gods, according to Gnostic thought, had more comprehensive plans. This is the burden of the rest of this book.

[12] Snider Howard M. – <u>Jesus or Christ</u>, Infinity Press, Conshohoken, Pa. 2009

[13] See the summary of Hoeller's work in Chapter 10

[14] See Edith Hamilton – <u>Mythology</u>; Grand Central Publishing, NY 1969.

[15] ibid

CHAPTER 7

Gnosticism: An Introduction

In three earlier books I attempted to describe the world views of Greco-Roman-Hebrew cultures that were significant in the formation of the New Testament.

In addition to these three world views impinging on Saul and other writers of the New Testament there was a fourth significant strain of thought. This was attractive to many intellectuals who had a general interest in spirituality or supernatural spiritual knowledge. There were many diverse and confusing forms of these philosophical-religious ideas but they may be subsumed under the term Gnosticism.

This system of thought encompasses a host of ideas, concepts and terms many of which are intertwined. Gnostic groups have speculated about the unknowable supernatural realm with its Gods and spirits. They have constructed varied and even contradictory conceptions of supernatural spiritual beings and their activities in this world and the heavens.

Elements of Gnosticism are still present and formative for the world view of modern groups such as Rosicrucians, Masons, orthodox Christian groups, particularly radical protestant evangelicals, fundamentalists in the Christian, Jewish and Muslim traditions and even right wing religious-political groups in various societies.

However one common element of Gnosticism is the certainty that under specific conditions, knowledge, wisdom and power of the supernatural world are available to human beings.

The term Gnosticism comes from the Greek word for knowledge; *gnosis*. (γνῶσις). It refers to esoteric consciousness, which is claimed by Gnostics to be the key to unlocking transcendent understanding, self-realization, and/or unity with God.[16]

The complexity of the qualities of gnosis are expressed by the following disconnected collection of words and phrases provided by some scholars.

"Completely perfect in light, Enlightenment, Limitless, Unsearchable, Immeasurable, Incomprehensible, Incorruptible, Ineffable, Invisible, Unnamable and Eternal. This ultimate Spiritual reality is superior to Perfection, Blessedness and Divinity." (New World Encyclopedia; see the article on agnosticism, section-creation)

Gnostics generally believe they can acquire this esoteric knowledge in the personal, individual search for increased spirituality. It is expected that the practitioners of meditation and contemplation, will come to know supernatural spirituality, often referred to as God, in some increased way and thus participate in a greater portion of the spirit and power of the supernatural world.

Those who persist in this search will acquire an increasing level of spirituality. Consequently these spiritualized human beings will be less attached to the fleshly concerns of other human beings in this world.

The process is reciprocal. As they become increasingly spiritual they will know and understand themselves more fully.

Gnosticism: A definition

For the purposes of this book I have developed a definition which makes sense in the context of the "esoteric knowledge" dimension of the meaning of the word gnosis.

Any one who is convinced they have the truth about what their God does and wants is by definition, at least in this book, a Gnostic. If any human being thinks they have supernatural spiritual knowledge they are a Gnostic. Anyone claiming to know anything about the supernatural world and its spirits is a Gnostic. Any human being who knows what God wants them and other human beings to do and think is a Gnostic!

There are multitudes of preachers, and other people, proclaiming doctrines of Gnosticism, particularly Dualistic Gnosticism in our society. I would refer you to "Christian" radio and television preachers for overwhelming supportive data.

Time and regions of the origin of Gnosticism

There is little agreement among scholars relative to these topics. Some believe that Christianity and Gnosticism arose at the same time and in the same regions and thus demonstrate some degree of mutual influence.

Other scholars hold that Gnostic thought arose at different times in different cultures in the ancient world. Some believe that Zoroastrianism, with its dualistic thought, developing in the region of ancient Persia more than two millennia BCE, generated ideas which appear in Gnostic doctrines common in many cultures through many centuries since that time.

I find this Zoroastrian source perspective to be most helpful in an understanding of similar thoughts of far Eastern cultures, the Old Testament, classic Greek philosophers, Neo-Platonism, the work of Philo of Alexandria in the second century BCE, the New Testament and powerful people today, who appeal to their Gods in support of their religious and religious-political doctrines.

If this perspective is accepted a few observations may be pertinent. This early origin of Gnosticism allows for Eastern and Western variations. These two divisions have different emphases.

The Eastern division emphasizes the disciplined meditative life and the search for the universal principles by which human beings should live.

This division contained two somewhat different perspectives. One of these perspectives is represented by Buddhism. The other division is represented by Daoism (Taoism), a significant philosophy of North East Asia. The common symbol of this system is a wheel with two overlapping and inclusive opposed characteristics.

A paraphrase of a twentieth century poem, attributed to Lovelace, reflects a modern literary version of this thought system in the following way.

> There is so much bad in the best of us,
> And so much good in the worst of us,
> It ill behooves the most of us,
> To criticize the rest of us!

Elements of Western Gnosticism, particularly those influencing the Bible, are discussed in following chapters.

CHAPTER 8

Core Doctrines of Western Gnosticism[17]

Through the centuries variations also arose in the western division, with modifications, additions and much confusion.

There were two major varieties of Gnosticism common in the Near East and Southern Europe at the beginning of our era; Monistic and Dualistic Gnosticism.

The following concise summaries of these two systems of Gnostic thought emphasize their major points of contention. These points of contention are sufficiently intensive to suggest that these two groups of Gods and their adherents are in conflict. The conflict is known as the "War of the Gods."

Remember the words God and Gods are interchangeable!

Monistic Gnosticism (Pure Spirit Gods, Ultimate Unity)

*Monistic Gnosticism understands that supernatural spirituality is the only **true reality**.

*Supernatural spirits dwell in the **world of the spirits**

*These supernatural spirits are the only **Gods;** hence the name Monistic Gods. [18]

*This God is **good.**

*This good God is **timeless**. There is no past or future. There is no such thing as time. There is only timeless eternity.

44

*This God **created nothing.**

*Before the beginning of time this good, total spirit God; this Ultimate Unity God, decreed that any non-spiritual thing, any **physical creation is "flesh."**

*Flesh is a condition of **"ignorance of supernatural spirituality."**

*Ignorance of supernatural spirituality is the essence of **evil.**

*Spirits that create anything physical are **evil.**

*Evil as represented in physical creation would produce **corruption, deterioration and destruction.**

* Physical creation is an **illusion.**

But physical creation occurred

How could such a thing happen?

According to Gnostic thought various emanations emerged from the Monistic God. These were spirits of various kinds: Aeons, Elohim, Demiurges, Christs, Demigods, Avatars, etc. From certain perspectives any of these, in some way, represent all the others. There were many generations of these spirits. (30 in some traditions, 10 in the Jewish kabbalistic system).

> "True the basic Gnostic myth has many variations, but all of these refer to Aeons, intermediate deific beings who exist between the ultimate spirit and ourselves."[19]

In Gnostic thought spiritual beings and spiritual classes of beings were in existence before time or anything physical was created. Spirit was all there was ineternity; the timeless era before time was created by the Elohim.

Some of these emanations in defiance of the Monistic God's decree began to do non-spiritual things.

Dualistic Gnosticism (the Creator Gods)

In Gnostic thought the following items are crucial.

*The Elohim created **time.**

*The Elohim created the **physical universe,** hence the name "Creator God."

*As a result there are now **two realities:** spiritual reality and physical reality; hence the name "**Dualistic Gods.**"

*The Creator God created human beings. They are physical and therefore "**flesh.**"

*Human beings are "flesh" and therefore **ignorant of supernatural spiritual knowledge**. This is consistent with the Monistic Gods' characterization of "flesh

*Humans, as a consequence of this ignorance, are **evil.**

*The Creator Gods dwell in the **world of the spirits** but, on occasion, they send their representatives (Angels, Christs, Avitars, etc.) to their created world to do things to and with their creation.

*The Creator Gods characterize themselves with the **spiritual qualities** which had been claimed by the Monistic Gods.
*The Creator God declared all Creation to be **good**. This was a direct and deliberate affront to the Monistic God!

*Creation was an **act of defiance** against the Monistic Pure Spirit God.

*The Dualistic God declared the Monistic God to be **evil, bad**; even a **false God**.

*In Dualistic Gnostic thought, the Creator Gods are **superior** to the Monistic Gods in all respects.

*All the plans relative to physical creation and especially human beings were made by the Creator God **before time began and before the earth was created.**[20]

Which God is right? (righteous) (Romans 3:21-26)

This is, in Gnosticism, the fundamental question of the universe, in both its spiritual and physical dimensions. It is also the primary question of the Bible. This question provides the singular framework for the literature of the Bible, probably even the reason for its existence.

Had the Creator Gods done the right thing in creating the physical universe and its human beings or was the Monistic God right in declaring all "flesh" to be evil? Which God is good? Which God is bad? Which God is right. (righteous)

The reaction of Monism to Dualism

*Monistic Gnosticism recognized what the Creator Gods had done. Their doctrine relative to this matter is clear in the following reference.

> "Pure Spirit, (the Monistic God) is set in stark contrast to the Old Testament Creator-God; a Demiurge. This Demiurge created the universe and every thing in it. This Creator God is not the true God."[21]

Theologians and Bible scholars have been almost exclusively "general Christians" (Christians of all stripes!)." They struggle to explain the nature of God and God's spirit. They have studied the Bible from many perspectives but have failed to look at it from a perspective which gives serious attention to the social creation of knowledge.

By the second century Monistic Gnosticism was a significant movement in the early Church. It was so powerful that it posed a real alternative to the doctrines of the Roman bishops who are described as "proto-orthodox" by some modern scholars.

These bishops, from the second to fourth centuries, quoted Monistic Gnostic doctrines in their written work hoping to refute them. They denounced Monistic Gnostics as heretics and their doctrines as heresy. For them the words heretic and Gnostic were melded into one intellectual construct.

These bishops, in their own minds, had the ultimate truths about supernatural spiritual knowledge and encapsulate them in their doctrines. Hence, in their self perceptions, they had the truth. Therefore they could not be heretics. Since they were not heretics they could not be Gnostics.

But these bishops had their own mental constructs, their own speculative descriptions, their own doctrines about the supernatural spirits and their relationships with human beings. Their doctrines about such matters were, for them, absolute truths. They had their own extended version of supernatural spiritual knowledge. Consequently they were Gnostics in any careful, consistent use of the word.

It is true they were not Monistic Gnostics. But they were Gnostics according to massive testimony in the Bible. They were Dualistic Gnostics. (Creator God Gnostics) They defined their particular set of doctrines relative to the supernatural world as incontrovertible truth: the Word of God and the Holy Scriptures."

With this kind of designation and endorsement their doctrines, from their viewpoint, could not be heretical and therefore could not be Gnosticism. The orthodox Churchmen and their followers for two thousand years have not been able to recognize the real nature of their intellectual constructs. Are Christian Bible scholars, even in academia equally blind?

Competition for adherents

At the time the New Testament was being produced, these two kinds of supernatural spiritualities, these Gnosticisms, were in competition for adherents.

Significant elements of Monistic doctrine persisted among segments of philosophically-oriented thinkers who also were attracted by selected doctrines and ethical dimensions of the emerging Christian churches. These thinkers and their doctrines became prominent in some of Paul's churches and became strong competitors of Dualistic Christian Gnosticism and its proto-orthodox leaders.

By the middle of the second century CE, Monistic Christians were denounced as heretics and violently oppressed, particularly by proto-orthodox Roman bishops.[22]

One of the most prominent of these heretics was Marcion of Sinope.

Dualistic Gnosticism predominates in the Western World

The above described Gnosticisms were both present in Christianity in the early centuries of our era. But only Monistic Gnosticism was labeled as "Gnosticism," condemned as heresy and cruelly persecuted almost to the point of extinction.

Most cultures in the Western World, since the fourth century, have been committed to Creator God Dualistic Gnosticism. This world view is the dominant view of the Old Testament, the New Testament, the most powerful Apostolic and ante-Nicene Fathers and Christianity to the present day. However their doctrines are not known as Gnosticism. They are known as Christian orthodoxy in its various versions of Catholic and Protestant traditions.[23]

---

[16] New World Encyclopedia-Gnosticism. The Encyclopedia Brittanica – Gnosticism.

[17] The elements of Gnostic beliefs in this chapter are indicated in direct quotes, paraphrases or summaries from various sources. (See the extended work of Stephen A Hoeller[17] in footnote 32 following)
[18] Wikipedia.org/wiki/monism – An extensive article discussing various aspects of Gnostic monism. Consult the Glossary - God entry
[19] On the internet search for Gnosticism. There are many sources. Among these I have found a number that were most helpful. Most quotations in this chapter are from these sources. (a) Gnosticism The Free University (b)The Gnostic world View: a Brief Summary of Gnosticism (c) New World Encyclopedia/Gnosticism. (d)Encyclopedia Brittanica/Gnosticism - see The Cosmos section (e) Wikopedia www.gnosis,org/gnintro.**html**
[20] See Appendix G
[21] en.wikopedia.org/wiki/Gnosticism#the_main_features
[22] Erhman, Bart – DVD-From Jesus to Constantine, Lecture 18
[23] Ibid – all the lectures.

CHAPTER 9

The Creation of Time and the World

"... his works were finished from the foundation of the world." (Hebrews 4:3)

There are a number of doctrines which are crucial to the world view of Gnosticism. The concept and unique meaning of the terms "knowledge" and "flesh" were treated in the preceding chapters and reappear in following chapters.

Two other Biblical and Gnostic realities appeared at the moment of creation. One was time. The other was physical creation. These realities, like all of God's plans, were designed in the timeless eternity before time began and before the "foundation of the world was laid."

"In the beginning God created the heavens and the earth" (Genesis 1:1)

In the beginning of time God created time and the physical universe. Humans know about these two things. We know nothing about any supernatural spiritual realities.

"Before time" and "before creation" like "knowledge" and "flesh" are foundational concepts of Gnosticism. They appear in many enigmatic Biblical passages, particularly in the New Testament. An appreciation of all these doctrines is essential to an understanding of Gnosticism, particularly Dualistic Gnosticism.

We live in the context of these two realities but have never been told why they exist or what their ultimate purpose might be. The purposes of these realities have been a mystery hidden by the Creator God since the beginning of time. But the purposes were revealed, according to the New Testament writers, in the first century CE. Consequently information about these realities is an underlying theme in much of the New Testament.

> "...Of this gospel I was made a minister...to make all men see what is the plan of the mystery hidden for ages in God who created all things; that through the church the manifold wisdom of God might now be made known to the principalities and powers in the heavenly places. This was according to the eternal purpose..." (Ephesians 3:7-11)

However Bible readers have been mystified by this material due to the fact that the Bible presents this information from the perspective of Creator God Gnosticism. The quotations in this chapter are only a few such Gnostic doctrines.

None of this hidden material makes sense from a scientific world view. But if one knows about the fundamental assumptions of the Biblical version of Creator God Gnosticism an intriguing view of a timeless eternity emerges. Eternity is interrupted by an interlude of time. This interlude of time was designed by the Creater God for a supernatural purpose. A startling explanation of the purposes of the ages is revealed. Let us look at the rudiments of these ideas.

The beginning of time is coincidental with the creation of the world and the beginning of the ages. Prior to this there was no such thing as time or a physical universe. There was only timeless spirit. This timeless spirit is known in Gnosticism as Monistic Gods or Ultimate Unity or Transcendental Spiritual

Unity and a whole range of their spiritual emanations: gods, demi-gods, Elohim and other spirits.

The Elohim interrupted timeless eternity with the creation of time and the physical universe including their crowning creation: human beings. At this point the myths concerning the ancient world turned serious attention to the activities of humans beings and their relationships to the Gods.

The Gods are always timeless. Time is a variable of interest and value only to human beings.

Consequently if we wish to partition time into ages we must use human variables. Human beings have always considered the more traumatic changes in their social life as points of transition from one age to another. All major cultures of the ancient world have stories about such changes. These are the ages or epochs of human cultures. However the Gods in all cases are close by.

The ages represented in the Old Testament seem to be drawn from early Assyrian and Egyptian myths. From these sources the writers developed stories relevant to their own interests, purposes and perspectives.

There are various ways in which time in the ancient world may be divided into ages. In a broad stroke way, it seems reasonable to find the following ages in the Old Testament myths. The age of Adam, ending with the expulsion from Eden. The age of the patriarchs in two phases: the first ending with the flood and the second ending with the confusion of languages at Babel. The age of Abraham and the Children of Israel ending with the Exodus and finally, the age of the Hebrew people in Palestine with mini-ages marked by periods of foreign domination.

This last age of the Old Testament came to an end in the first century CE with the revelation of the "hidden mystery of God" to all the Pauls and other writers who report this received knowledge in the New Testament. This transition event, from the Christian view point, was ultimately significant for every human being in the world. Life and destiny for all the rest of time and eternity is now determined by their response to the crucifixion!

This ultimately significant event was the pivotal point of the first part of the "plan of the mystery" which had been hidden in all the ages since time began.

This was a complex of plans designed by the Elohim God (the Creator Gods) in the eternity before they had created either time or the physical universe. These plans were established before the ages began! The Creator Gods ordained that all aspects of the plans would be executed automatically, at the appropriate times, in the time of the ages.

Time, physical Creation and human beings were all prerequisites for the execution of this eternal plan.

It was a plan in which Christ Jesus, the only begotten son of the Creator God would play a final pivotal role. This aspect of the plan is known in our age as the plan of salvation. And this crucial event is followed by the activation of the "plan of spiritualization."

These plans would indeed affect human beings, but that was irrelevant to their real purpose. The Creator God made the plans for his own eternal purpose. The plan was designed to deal with a problem which had emerged in the realm of the spirits in the eternity before the creation of time or the world.

"...the gospel is the power of God, who saved us and called us with a holy calling, not in virtue of our works but in virtue of his own purpose and the grace which he gave us ages ago." (2nd Timothy 1:9)

What was God's "own purpose?"

If we are going to understand these mystifying materials in the New Testament we must come to grips with such passages. God created time and the world for "his own purposes. And these purposes, from the Christian perspective, were revealed in the first and second centuries of our age.

The Creator God, who is an all knowing God, knew his plan would affect human beings at various stages through the ages. Some would be beneficial but such human benefits were not the purpose of the plan. Any benefit to human beings was only an irrelevant side effect, an effect which the writer of the Timothy document describes as a graceful action. Timothy attempts to make it relevant to human beings but distorts the essence of the revelation which he claims to have received.

It could have been of benefit to people of previous ages. But the only message they heard from God, during those ages, was the demand to be obedient. The benefit was available only to those human beings who "obeyed." No human being obeyed, not even one.

"...the message which they heard did not benefit them, because it did not meet with faith in the hearers. For we who have believed enter that rest, as he has said, 'as I swore in my wrath, they shall never enter my rest' although his works were finished from the foundation of the world. For he has somewhere spoken of the seventh

56

day in this way, 'and God rested on the seventh day from all his works.'" (Hebrews 4:3)

The Creator Gods had designed all aspects of these plans before time began. Their work was "finished from the foundation of the world." God rested when he finished creation and has never gone back to work!

The Bible is explicit about this matter. The Creator God after finishing creation did nothing more. In all the ages, including our age, the Creator God has done nothing and will do nothing.

The plan was set in motion by the creation of time and physical creation. All the events in the plan were activated with a foreordained, prescribed, outcome during all the ages of time.

But now at the end of all the preceding ages and the beginning of our age the plans of salvation and spiritualization were revealed and activated.

Some human beings believe in the plans. The result for them is "rest." And with them and their faith the age of the church began.

At the proper time the plans were manifested in the preaching of Titus (the reactionary Paul) as he claims. But there were many other preachers, beginning with authentic Paul who preached at the proper time about many aspects of this mystery which had been hidden until this new age had arrived.

"...to further the faith of God's elect and the knowledge of the truth which accords with godliness, in hope of eternal life, which God, who never lies, promised ages ago and at the proper time manifested in his word through the preaching with which I have been entrusted..." (Titus 1:2)

Why did this reactionary Paul make the point that God never lies? Titus is obviously a Creator God Gnostic. From that view point there were other Gods who were liars and false gods. The Monistic Gods, from the Dualistic Gnostic perspective, are the prime example.

We must remember that the Creator Gods rested at the conclusion of creation and did nothing more. But a supernatural being, who was not an emanation but rather the only begotten son of the Creator God, Christ Jesus had his crucial part to play-the crucifixion. This would occur at the end of the age and mark the beginning of a new age; the age of the church.

The writer of Hebrews casts "Christ Jesus" in the role of a supernatural high priest who is at the same time a supernatural sacrifice.

If he had been a human,

> "...then he would have had to suffer repeatedly from the foundation of the earth."

> "but as it is he appeared once for all at the end of the age..." (Hebrew 9:26)

He was a preordained supernaturally designated spiritual sacrifice to assuage the wrath of his father toward his disobedient human creation. We must remember that the Creator God never loved his disobedient crowning creation. His attitude had been "wrathful" toward them from the moment of their disobedience in the age of Adam at the beginning of time.

The wrath of God may have been "assuaged" with the sacrifice at Calvary but God never "loved the human race." He had created them for other purposes.

The myth of God loving human beings did not appear until the concept was constructed in a preliminary way called justice by a few ethically oriented Old Testament prophets, Monistic Gnostics and some New Testament writers, particularly John in his gospel of the second century.

However the crucifixion ended the multiple ages of God's wrathful relationship with human beings. This is true for those who have faith in the plans.

It also initiated our era, the church age which began with the revelation experienced by Saul of Tarsus. Subsequently the other Pauls and some other writers of the New Testament reported on further revelations respecting the impact of the "church" on the supernatural world.

> "...and to make all men see what is the plan of the mystery hidden for ages, who created all things; that through the church the manifold wisdom of God, might be known to the principalities and powers in the heavenly places. This was according to the eternal purpose which he has realized in Christ Jesus." (Ephesians 3:9-11)

The real purpose for the creation of human beings is explicitly stated. The purpose of human beings in this world is clarified beyond a shadow of doubt in this passage.

> "...through the church the manifold wisdom of God, might be known to the principalities and powers in the heavenly places."

When the principalities and powers in the heavenly places finally know the manifold wisdom of God will time come to an end? Will timeless eternity resume? Does Gnosticism have an answer to this question?

CHAPTER 10

Gnosticism: Similarities and Differences

The most crucial similarities and differences between the two dominant Gnosticisms are indicated in the preceding Chapters.

There are other aspects of Gnosticism which might be categorized as secondary but still important underlying conceptions. Several of these are briefly summarized in this chapter which also contains several important references to documents by individuals who are writing from a Monistic or Dualistic Gnostic perspective. These may enlarge an understanding of their influences on Christianity. Bible readers and Bible scholars might detect similarities and differences with their own beliefs.

The Church Fathers, (Irenaeus, Ignatius, Justin Martyr, Tertullian and others, from the mid second century into the fourth century CE), in their anti-heresy writings, quoted extensively from what they defined as Gnostic materials. These anti-heresy materials and many other religious documents were collected together and published in 1885. (See the 10 volume set of writings by the Ante-Nicene Fathers.)

Some writings of Monistic Gnostic Christians escaped destruction but were forced underground. In recent years some have been recovered from various sites. One of the most important of these is the excavations at Nag-Hammadi, Egypt in 1945.[24] Thirteen, leather bound, codices of second century materials have been found. From these sources scholars have been able to reconstruct the basic Monistic Gnostic philosophical and religious ideas as well as other stories and purported sayings of Jesus.

Neo-Platonic ideas of the first century were closely associated with elements of Gnostic fundamentals. Ideas similar to neo-Platonism and the Alexandrian philosopher Philo influenced early Christianity.

The New Testament, especially the authentic epistles of Paul, the work of pseudonymous Pauls and the writings of Luke contain Gnostic phrases and reflect many foundational Gnostic beliefs.

Marcionism,– Marcion came from Sinope, Pontus, Asia Minor, where his father was a Bishop.[25] He moved to Rome and pursued a career as a Christian church leader. He was considered to be the most important Christian theologian in the time period between Paul and the Apostolic Fathers. His theological perspectives tended to support Monistic Gnosticism. Consequently proto-orthodox Latin Bishops denounced him as *"The Christian Gnostic Heretic."*

He acquired an extensive and powerful following and became a threat to other church leaders of his time. These leaders condemned him, destroyed his writings and persecuted his followers. His Gnostic Christian churches were forced to the margins of early Christian thought. Marcion died about 160 CE.

But there is one authentic surviving Marcion document: Antithesis. It is probably the best summary of Monistic Gnosticism which existed during the years in which the New Testament materials were being circulated in the emerging Christian churches. A summary of its crucial points follows.[26]

"(1) The Creator of the world, although a real God, must be distinguished from the higher God, unknown except as he was revealed in Christ; (2) The Creator of the world is a just God, but severe and harsh; the God whom Christ revealed is a Father, a God of love; (3) judgment is the prerogative of the Creator; redemption is the free gift of the God of love; (4) the Jewish scriptures represent a true revelation of the Creator, but they do not speak of or for the God whom alone Christians ought to worship and from whom alone salvation from the present wicked world is to be received; (5) the revelation in Christ was intended not merely to supplement or 'fulfill' Judaism but entirely to displace it–the one had no connection with the other; (6) the Son of the Father did not actually take sinful flesh but only appeared to do so; (7) there is no resurrection of the flesh; and (8) Paul was the only true apostle, to whom Christ committed his gospel–other 'apostles' were false and had misled the church.[27]

Item 8 provides absolute evidence that Paul was considered to be a Monistic Gnostic by Marcion of Sinope, the prominent "Christian heretic" of the second century.

Monistic Gnosticism is far from dead. Note part b of Items 1 2 3 & 4 above. These statements are foundational for most Christians and are central to Marcion's heretical Monistic Gnosticism. But when it comes to doctrines of crucifixion, salvation, spirituality and supernatural rewards, Christians worship the Dualistic Gnostic God and his dictates in the Bible.

There are Monistic Gnostic groups all over the world. Many of them call themselves Christian churches.

One of the most prominent, modern American Monistic Gnostics is Stephen A Hoeller. (the self styled Bishop of Gnosticism.) He provides an excellent summary of earlier Gnostic doctrines which are still common in the 21st century.

Teaching and Doctrinal Orientation [28]

By Stephen A Hoeller

"While the ancient Gnostic teachers were very pluralistic and creative regarding the details of their teachings and practices, at the same time they embraced a set of common assumptions which form the core of the Gnostic tradition. The model of reality shown forth in the Gnostic scriptures and in the Gnostic tradition may be very briefly (and therefore somewhat inadequately) outlined by way of the following points:

1   *There is an original and transcendental spiritual unity which came to emanate a vast manifestation of pluralities.*

2   *The manifest universe of matter and mind (psyche) was not created by the original spiritual unity but by spiritual beings possessing inferior powers These creators possessing inferior powers have as one of their objectives the perpetual separation of humans from the unity (God).*

3   *The human being is a composite, the outer aspect being the handiwork of the inferior creators, while the "inner man" has the character of a fallen spark of the ultimate divine unity.*

4   *The fallen sparks of transcendental holiness slumber in their material and mental prison, their self-awareness stupefied by forces of materiality and mind.*

5   *The slumbering sparks have not been abandoned by the ultimate unity, rather there is a constant effort forthcoming from this unity that is directed toward their awakening and liberation.*

6   *The awakening of the inmost divine essence in humans is effected by salvific knowledge, called Gnosis.*

7   *Salvific knowledge, or Gnosis, is not brought about by belief, or the performance of virtuous deeds, or by obedience to commandments, for these can at best but serve as preparatory circumstances leading toward liberating knowledge.*

8   *Among the helpers of the slumbering sparks a particular position of honor and importance belongs to a feminine emanation of the unity. The name of this emanation is Sophia (Wisdom). She was involved in the creation of the world and ever since remained the guide of her orphaned human children.*

9   *From the earliest times of history, messengers of light have been sent forth from the ultimate unity. The task of these messengers has ever been the advancement of Gnosis in the souls of humans.*

10 *The greatest of these messengers in our historical and geographical matrix was the descended Logos of God, manifesting in Jesus Christ.*

11 *Jesus exercised a twofold ministry: He was a teacher, imparting instruction concerning the way of Gnosis, and he was a hierophant, imparting mysteries.*

12 *The mysteries imparted by Jesus (which are also known as sacraments) are mighty aids toward Gnosis and have been entrusted by him to his apostles and to their successors"*

13 *By way of the spiritual practice of the mysteries (sacraments) and by a relentless and uncompromising striving for Gnosis, humans can steadily advance toward liberation from all confinement, material and otherwise."*

The materials from these and other sources are complex. But there is one universal and persistent feature. The supernatural spiritual world communicates with, and provides knowledge (esoteric knowledge) to some human beings. Conversely human beings can communicate with the supernatural world, and experience the processes of spiritualization.[29]

The nameless God

In the stories of the Children of Israel, Moses had adopted the JHWH tradition of his Midianite father-in-law. He seems to have found something of an Abrahamic theology in the Negev. This has marvelous overtones consistent with later Gnostic thought.

> "What is your name…God said to Moses I am who I am…the God of Abraham has sent me to you." (Exodus 3:13-16)

This is a nameless God whom Moses did not see; a God who is pure spirit and therefore invisible but symbolized in fire and flames. Moses was an emissary of this God. This "I Am" God tradition persisted into the New Testament.

> "Jesus said to them, 'Truly truly I say to you, before Abraham was 'I am'" (John 8:58).

This "Jesus" is John's spiritualized Jesus, perhaps something like Paul's Jesus Christ, the product of a hundred years of myth creation.

The spark of divinity

Despite all the emphasis on evil most Gnostics believe that the Creator God as well as the Monistic God provided human beings with an element of the divine essence; a hint of supernatural spirituality.

The Monistic Gnostic view

See Hoellers items 7-9 above.

"The explanation of this state through the use of a complex mythological-cosmological drama in which a divine element 'falls' into the material realm and lodges itself within certain human beings; from here, it may be returned to the divine realm through a process of awakening (leading towards salvation). The salvation of the individual thus mirrors a concurrent restoration of the divine nature; a central Gnostic innovation was to elevate individual redemption to the level of a cosmically-significant event.[30]

The Dualistic Gnostic view

"God created man in his own image, in the image of God He created…them." (Genesis 1:27 KJV)

Salvation and spiritualization are certainly cosmically-significant events. Jesus Christ came from the supernatural spiritual world and by virtue of the incarnation and crucifixion saves human beings. The Holy Spirit enters into some human beings, provides knowledge of the supernatural world and as a consequence these human beings become supernaturally spiritual. This is Dualistic Gnosticism at the core of Christianity.

The process of awakening (enlightenment) mentioned in the above quotation is discussed at length in later chapters under the general title of **spiritualization.**

The good and the bad

These words recur in the preceding chapter and the solution to evil is the topic of the next chapter. They require some further discussion.

It must be noted that the authentic Paul's writings, at least in the English translations confuses the distinction between "evil" and "sin" and uses these words interchangeably.

In Monistic thought the terms good and bad have no relationship to modern ideas of morality or ethics. The good in Monistic Gnosticism is knowledge of supernatural spirituality. The bad (evil) is ignorance of supernatural spirituality.

In Dualistic Gnosticism this matter of supernatural spiritual knowledge is also of major importance; but only under certain conditions.

According to the Garden of Eden story, humans were created ignorant of supernatural spiritual knowledge and the Creator God wanted to keep them that way. He also made them with the power of choice and later warned them about the consequences of disobedience. Adam made the wrong choice and determined the fate of all descendents. Forever after, the choice of which God they worshipped and how they obeyed became a paramount marker of goodness or badness.

Although Dualistic Gnosticism emphasizes the same point, there is much more than supernatural spiritual knowledge or ignorance of such knowledge that falls in the categories of good or bad.

In addition, what is good or bad is culturally-dependent and variable over time. The selection of the God to be worshipped, in theistic religions, is crucial. And obedience is the moral touchstone. In ritualistic religions, the proper performance is the mark of the good person. In communal kinds of religion, the consequences of interpersonal relations are either good or bad and the actors so categorized.

Dualistic morality, bad (evil) and good, emerged at the creation of time and the physical universe. In Dualistic Gnosticism, both good and bad (evil) exist in the supernatural spiritual world and the created world. There are good and bad spirits; also good and bad humans. The Bible is a remarkable source of information about these moral and spiritual realities.

These profound earthly and cosmic problems have bothered the Gods and human beings since the beginning of time. Who is responsible for all the evil in the supernatural world and in this human world?. How are these problems of evil and sin to be solved?

Human evil: who is responsible?

The words flesh, evil and sin are crucial words in The New Testament.

The first two are significant ear-marks of Gnostic thought and exclusively relevant to the ignorance of supernatural spiritual knowledge.

Human beings are flesh, therefore ignorant of such knowledge and thus evil.

In Gnostic thought there are two explanations for the origins of evil in our world.

The view point of Monistic Gnosticism.

The pure Spirit God sometimes called Ultimate Unity is the Monistic God who decreed that any non-spiritual thing, any physical creation is flesh. The basic characteristic of flesh is ignorance of supernatural spirituality. This ignorance is the source of all evil. Any spirits that create flesh are also evil.

The Creator God, the Dualistic God created the physical universe and, from this viewpoint, is therefore evil. He also created human beings. These human beings are flesh, ignorant of supernatural knowledge and therefore evil. Obviously the Creator God is responsible for both these dimensions of evil.

The view point of Dualistic Gnosticism

The Creator God had two conclusive proofs that he was not responsible for evil in our world.

The first proof: The Dualistic God was aware that his crowning creation were flesh but by his own decree flesh was good, not evil. The element that was evil in the creation drama was the Monistic God's arbitrary decree. Therefore the Monistic God was responsible for evil in this world.

But there is a complicating variable as we weigh this evidence.

The Dualistic God had developed a plan, before time began, that would involve the salvation of human beings from their evil (ignorance of supernatural spirituality) and thus prove that the Monistic God could finally not enforce his decree. But this would take time. Therefore the Creator God allowed the Monistic God's decree to stand.

The second proof: The Dualistic God had created humans with the capacity to make bad choices and the tendency to do so. They were created also with the capacity and tendency to disobey his commandments. Bad choices and disobedience were both evil when these choices involved the worship of Gods other than their creator which they did repeatedly from the beginning of time. Therefore human beings were responsible for evil in this World.

There is a third point of view unrelated to Gnosticism.

The view point of human beings and the problem of sin

Human beings have no knowledge of the supernatural spiritual world. They are ignorant of the machinations of supernatural spirits.

Human beings know only about themselves, other individuals, groups of other humans and their behaviors. These actions are human social interactions and are expressions of cultural mores which are time bound. Immoral behaviors are defined, in human communities, as sin; a big problem for humans and human societies. Obviously human beings are responsible for sin in this world.

But Gnosticism and its Gods are concerned only about "evil." They are not concerned about "sin." Sin is exclusively a human problem.

Does all this resolve the problem? Who really is responsible; the Gods or humans?

Regardless of these scenarios most extreme Gnostics believe:

> "The blame for the world's failings lies not with humans but with the God(s.)"[31]

70

The other God of course!

If this is the case we are left with the unresolved question; which God is really responsible for evil? The two relevant classes of Gods, since time began, have been in conflict about this matter. The New Testament, if its Gnostic dimensions are recognized, may provide the answer.

This is the central concern of the rest of this book.

[24] Encyclopedia Britannica - Gnosticism
[25] www.earlychristianwritings,com/marcion
[26] Ibid See section - Marcion and Marcionite Gnosticism
[27] Ibid
[28] en,wikipedia.org/wiki/Stephen A Hoeller
[29] Wikipedia.org/wiki/ Gnosticism – is an extended article crucial to an elementary understanding of this complex, confusing and often contradictory philosophical-religious system of thought. (the content box early in the article provides a table of contents)
[30] en.wikipedia.org/wiki/gnosticism
[31] www.gnosis,org/gnintro.htm (see The Deity section)

CHAPTER 11

Human Evil and Sin: the Solution [32]

The problem of evil reviewed

Evil (human ignorance of supernatural spirituality) and sin are both real problems for human beings. We grapple with their effects, individually and corporately. Both classes of Gnostic Gods have a solution to these problems.

In either case supernatural spiritualization is required. But the way in which human beings become supernatural spiritual beings is markedly different. There may be some overlap but consequences for human beings in the processes of becoming spiritual are worlds apart. This is a major aspect of the differences in Gnosticisms.

This is of particular concern for the Creator God. He had created them as flesh, therefore ignorant of supernatural spiritual knowledge and consequently evil. He must, in some way, prove to the Monistic God that they are really not evil. He had pronounced them good at Creation, but they are still evil by the Monistic God's decree. Had he made a mistake?

The problem of sin

Sin is of no concern to the Monistic Gods; they did not create human beings. The Creator God had created human beings with the capacity and tendency to make bad choices, even the possibility of disobeying their creator.

In the context of Gnostic thought sin was an intervening problem. The most horrendous consequences for this condition, death and eternal suffering, had been decreed by the Creator God. Why did the Creator God do these things to human beings? Why?

As it turns out, in the context of Gnostic thought, all this provided a marvelous strategic opportunity for the Dualistic Creator Gods in their cosmic struggle with the Monistic Ultimate Unity Gods.

In anticipation of future chapters let me remind you of the following Gnostic reality.

The Monistic and Dualistic Gods had serious differences regarding the creation of physical reality.

The Creator God deliberately created the physical universe in defiance of the Monistic God. This precipitated the War of the Gods. He also created human being with the evil characteristic and the tendency to sin. This was part of a plan designed before the beginning of time.

Enlightenment:
The Monistic Gnostic solution for evil

In the Gnostic perspective the problem is not sin. The problem is ignorance of supernatural spirituality. This ignorance is the essence of evil. This can be solved only by becoming spiritual, supernaturally spiritual, and thereby spiritually knowledgeable. Meditation of the spiritual dimensions of reality over against the physical dimensions engages human beings with supernatural spiritual power. They become enlightened and supernaturally spiritual. This condition produces freedom from any concerns or limitations of the flesh.

The following quotation reflects the Monistic Gnostic perspective. Apart from the hostile anti-Creation God comments they also reflect many of the perspectives of Dualistic Gnosticism. Note the name calling tenor.

"Human nature mirrors the duality found in the world: in part it was made by the false Creator God and in part it consists of the light of the True God. Humankind contains a perishable physical component and a psychic, a spiritual component which is a fragment of the divine essence. This latter part is often symbolically referred to as the 'divine spark.'"[33]

"The myth conveys the message that the Biblical Creator is only a parody of divinity. Life in this imperfect world does contain inklings of truth; human wisdom does have a relation to divinity reality. Yet wisdom can go astray, and false gods can result. Humanity, in a state of spiritual amnesia before accepting the revelation of this myth, is awakened by reconnection with Perfect Knowledge".[34]

In both types of Gnosticism spiritual development lies in attaining "*gnosis*" kept secret to all but the initiated.

"Gnostics do not look to salvation from sin but rather from ignorance...ignorance...whereby is meant ignorance of spiritual realities is dispelled only by gnosis, and the decisive revelation of gnosis is brought by the "messengers of light," especially by Christ(s), the Logos of the True God"[35]

"From earliest time "Messengers of the Light" have come forth from the true God in order to assist humans in their quest for "gnosis."[36]

These messengers are christs. This knowledge has practical effects for the Gnostic believers in this world.

"Gnosticism embraces numerous general attitudes toward life: it encourages non-attachment and non-conformity to the world, a being in the world, but not of the world; a lack of egotism and a respect for the freedom and dignity of other beings. Nonetheless, it appertains to the intuition and wisdom of every individual Gnostic to distill from these principles individual guidelines for their personal application."[37]

"Rules, however, are not relevant to Salvation. That is brought about only by Gnosis. Morality therefore needs to be viewed primarily in temporal and secular terms; it is ever subject to changes and modifications in accordance with the Spiritual development of the individual."[38]

People who have developed spiritually are those who have been initiated into ultimate esoteric supernatural spiritual knowledge. At the pinnacle of this process humans become supernaturally spiritual. Although still being human with its degenerative fleshy characteristics, those characteristics no longer have any relevance or consequences.

This knowledge, this enlightenment liberates a person from moral constraints. Morality is of concern only in the domain of the condition of human spiritual ignorance. It is of no relevance in the domain and experience of supernatural spiritual knowledge.

Dualistic Gnostic solution for evil more complex

In spite of the similarities indicated in the preceding material; the solution of evil in Dualistic Gnosticism is a vastly more complex procedure than in the Monistic version.

Sin in this context is not a problem. It is a tool in the solution.

In Dualistic Gnosticism it is possible to escape both evil and the consequences of sin and become a spiritual being, even a supernatural spiritual being; a son of the Creator God who is pure spirit. But this requires a complex twostep process.

In the first place the problem of the consequences of sin must be solved. The Creator Gods developed the plan of salvation to solve this problem. The saved are freed from the consequences of their sin and will not be punished in hell when they die. But this is not sufficient to transform them into supernatural spirits and make them fit for association with the Creator Gods in a post-time eternity.

Neither is it adequate to prepare them for the ultimate purposes of the Creator Gods in the spirit world. But it is sufficient to make them recruits for the second crucial step.

The second step is the activation of the "plan of spiritualization." This is required to transform these recruits into supernatural spiritual beings. This is a process which modifies the crucial deficiency of human beings; their ignorance of supernatural spiritual knowledge. Such knowledge qualifies them to be engaged with the Creator Gods' cosmic purposes.

The plan of salvation and the plan of spiritualization, with all their details, are the crucial strategies of the Creator Gods in their battle with the Monistic Gods. They are also the processes by which human beings become supernaturally spiritual.

Paul in his seven letters demonstrates that he was knowledgeable about both these plans of the Creator God and was deeply involved in aspects of their implementation.

---

[32] The Gnosticism literature is expansive. I suggest a return to the extended article en.wikipedia.org/wiki/gnosticism

[33] www.gnosis,org/gnintro.htm (see The Human Being section)

[34] Encyclopedia Britanica Gnosticism

[35] www.gnosis,org/gnintro.htm (see Salvation section)

[36] ibid (See Salvation section)

[37] Ibid (see conduct section)

[38] Ibid

CHAPTER 12

Responses to the Crucifixion

Our knowledge of Jesus of Nazareth is limited. There is some evidence that such a man was born about 4 BCE and was executed about 30 CE. The New Testament myths might suggest the historicity of a few other possibilities. The following observations are reasonable reconstructions.

Jesus of Nazareth grew to maturity and was a full participant in the culture of the peasant villages of Galilee in Palestine. In his late twenties he began talking about the inequalities of the ridged stratification structure and the burden of traditional religious dogma. He gained a considerable following. The religious and political institutional authorities feared his leadership was producing a rebellious social movement so they executed him.

Crucifixion: Jesus' followers response

The followers of Jesus were distraught. Those, who had been most deeply influenced by his ministry struggled to make sense of his life, teachings and tragic death. They wondered why such a good man was so badly treated.

Those most deeply influenced by him, met together, weighed his ethics and learned to live in ways he had taught them.

Some Jewish people began to think he was the Messiah. Jesus' brother was one of these and he led a movement which developed into the Jerusalem church.

Different interpretations soon resulted in disagreements, antagonisms and social fragmentation. It was all a disturbing and confusing mystery!

The crucifixion: Saul's response

Saul of Tarsus knew very little about the life, ministry or crucifixion of Jesus of Nazareth. But Saul in his maturity, a number of years after the crucifixion, became aware of Jesus' followers and began to persecute them. He must then have learned that Jesus had been a social trouble maker. He would have endorsed the crucifixion.

Saul, pursuing his own religious commitments, persecuted, imprisoned and endorsed the execution of fellow Jews, who were followers of Jesus. This was an effort to reconvert them to the true religion. But he failed. The trauma of this failure led him to a fundamental re-evaluation of his life and convictions. Many questions were raised in his mind.

Who and what was this remarkable man, Jesus of Nazareth, who could inspire such stubborn and courageous followers? Was this Jesus more than a man? This was a real possibility. In the context of his Greco-Roman culture, Avatars, Christs and other kinds of spirits from the supernatural world came to this world, took human form and did things to and with human beings.

If Jesus of Nazareth was a God-Man why did God permit his messenger to be crucified? Why?

Why was he really crucified? Was there some deeper cosmic significance to the crucifixion; some ultimate purpose of the supernatural spiritual powers of the heavens? This was an intriguing possibility in the Gnostic system of thought which was a significant component of the intellectual culture of his elite social world.

Saul struggled with these questions. His mental anguish led to a wrenching emotional trauma, an utter confusion of his world view. For the following three years early in the 40s CE, in the Arabian Desert and Damascus, he thought about these questions. During this time he claims to have had visions and finally had some answers.

Saul concluded that Jesus of Nazareth was, in fact, an Avatar, an ambassador from the world of the spirits. This was, for Saul, a major transformation of cosmic proportions. In his mind, Saul converted the human Jesus of Nazareth into a supernatural messenger, a Christ consistent with the religious-philosophical thought of his Greco-Roman-Hebrew culture.

Having come to a radically different world view, Saul was forced to find an explanation for the crucifixion of Jesus of Nazareth, who was now for him a Christ, a messenger from his God. Why did his God permit this special messenger to be crucified? Why? And immediately an even more troubling question arose.

His Dualistic God, the Creator God, was also a timeless, all powerful and all knowing God. His God knew what was going on in the supernatural world and what other spirits were doing with the earth and its human beings. In this context his God must have deliberately caused the crucifixion or it would not have happened! It was an over powering conundrum. Why did God permit his messenger, his Christ to be crucified?

Saul's ruminations in the context of Gnostic thought reminded him of some crucial realities in the world of the spirits. The conflict between the Monistic Gods and the Creator Gods related to the nature of flesh.

Flesh in this context referred to two overriding concerns. One was the human ignorance of the supernatural spiritual world. The other was the universal human tendency to disobey and sin.

Saul became convinced that his God had plans to solve these problems. The crucifixion, he concluded, was the pivotal act in the plan of salvation. It was the instrument to solve the problem of human sin; at least the consequences of sin.

The problem of human ignorance of supernatural spirituality and its attendant evil, he concluded, could also be solved by the plan of spiritualization.

By the time Paul was writing his letters, in the sixth decade CE, he knew that both plans had transcendent purposes. He also knew that God would use the flesh condition of human beings to further his cosmic interests against the Monistic Gods.

Human beings had crucial preliminary parts to play before the cosmic drama's final denouement could be realized. The problem of sin was the initial concern. Its resolution was critical since it was the prerequisite to spiritualization which, under certain conditions, could follow.

For two decades Paul promoted his gospel, the plan of salvation, which enabled him to found churches and write at least seven letters: Romans, I&II Corinthians, Galatians, I Thessalonians, Philemon and Philippians. These letters, written in the decade of the 50s, in the first century CE became the foundation for the rest of the New Testament.

Paul, writing some 75 years before John, would have agreed that the crucifixion would benefit human beings and save them from perishing. (John 3:16) But for Paul that was merely a secondary consequence, almost an incidental side effect.

He had an alternate understanding of the crucifixion.

Surely the single, most poignant summary of the New Testament message is his statement:

> "For our sake he made him to be sin who knew no sin, so that in him we might become the righteousness of God." (II Corinthians. 5:21)

This statement sets forth two fundamental principles of Creator God Gnosticism.

The first principle: the Creator God made him (Jesus Christ) sin, who knew no sin. Paul explains that Jesus is not a sacrifice but rather an incarnation and therefore flesh and consequently evil from a Monistic Gnostic point of view.

The second principle: responds to the purpose of the incarnation and crucifixion:

> "so that ...we might become the righteousness of God."

How can we, mere human beings who are both evil and sinners, do anything to make God righteous?

This is astounding. It is an intriguing cosmic contradiction! How can sinners become the "righteousness" of God. Utterly incomprehensible!

But in the context of Creator God Gnosticism it is straight forward and absolutely logical.

In Paul's theology, Jesus (his Jesus Christ) was not an emanation. He was the "only begotten son" of the Creator

God. He could do no evil. He could not sin. But he was incarnated and consequently was like ordinary human beings.

And the Creator God had decreed that all creation was good. This was a direct rejection of the Monistic God's decree. The incarnation and crucifixion (really a single myth) was a pivotal step in the long process of proving the Monistic God to be wrong and the Dualistic God to be right (righteous).

How did Paul know all this?

In his letters to the churches he provided details of the plans of salvation and spiritualization which were the essential activities in the task of obtaining evidence to prove the Creator God to be right and the Monistic God to be wrong.

If one is aware of the Gnostic world view its system of thought, these plans and their purposes become a central concern of the New Testament?

CHAPTER 13

Why Sin?

The general orthodox understanding of the plan of salvation was reviewed in a fragmentary way, in preceding chapters. The initial impetus for that plan, it is generally assumed, is sin.

In the thought system of Gnosticism there is an alternate understanding of the plan of salvation which emphasizes the interests of the Creator Gods rather than the welfare of human beings.

Both Gnostic systems of thought have significant implications for human beings, but the purposes and consequences are different.

The Creation: The development of sin

The Creator Gods created time. They also created the physical universe. By the decree of the Monistic Gods such creation is flesh. Flesh, in the first place is ignorance of supernatural spiritual knowledge. This condition produces corruption, degeneration and destruction. Both these dimensions may be summed up in one word: Evil.

The Creator Gods deliberately withheld knowledge of the supernatural world from human beings. This is an evil condition. Is the Creator God responsible for the evil of his human beings?

The Creator God, being a jealous God, did not want his human creation to know anything about other Gods and spirits; particularly the transcendental Monistic Gods. He desperately wanted to keep them ignorant of these spiritual realities.

Human beings, since the beginning of time, have been curious about the unknown, including the nature and activity of an imagined or possible supernatural world. They have been curious about the supernatural spirits who might dwell there. They have craved and searched for ways to know. This is a fundamental human reality. The Creator God made human beings this way. They have acted on this inclination ever since the beginning of time.

The Prohibition

The Creator God had created human beings devoid of any supernatural spiritual knowledge and forbade them to seek this knowledge.

In spite of these arbitrary Godly actions, He directly and explicitly told human beings how such knowledge might be attained. In a contradictory action, He cautioned that any attempt to get this knowledge would have disastrous consequences for them.

> "But of the tree of the Knowledge of Good and Evil you shall not eat, for in the day you eat of it you shall die. (Genesis 2:17)

This knowledge was accessible. All they had to do was to eat the fruit of the tree of the knowledge of good and evil. This fruit was right there beside them in the Garden of Eden.

They already had knowledge of the good since that was the Creator God's self definition and they fellowshipped with him in the garden in the cool of the evening.

But they wanted more knowledge of the supernatural world. Apparently they wanted the knowledge of evil! Was this knowledge of the Monistic God? At least, this was the Dualistic God's perception of things. It was his secret and he did not want his creation to know about the Monistic God.

A little imagination might enable a reconstruction of a conversation between God and our progenitors about this matter.

God – *Eat the fruit of the knowledge tree and you will get knowledge. You want to know about the Spirit world? Why? You know about me. So you know the good. Why in the world would you want to know about evil?*

Adam – *Oh! So that is part of the Spirit World! Thank you, I've been wondering. Are there other Gods and Spirits there? What are they like? What do they do?"*

God – *That's my secret. It is all a mystery to you and that is the way it should be. I made you that way. Don't try to get any more knowledge. Just don't do it!*

Adam – *But I want to know. I must know! I have an uncontrollable compulsion to know; it is my basic nature and Eve has this same inclination.*

God – *Don't eat of that fruit! Don't disobey me.*

Eve –*But God, you made us this way. I feel exactly like Adam about this matter, but even more intensely.*

God – *I know that. But it's none of your business. I still forbid you to eat the fruit of the tree of the knowledge of good and evil. It's an order. If you disobey me I will banish you from Eden and punish you with death and other pains.*

Adam and Eve – *But, But!*

Given these realities would any normal human being ever have obeyed?

The Fall

They couldn't obey. The Creator God had also made them with the capacity and inclination to disobey.

They responded according to their fundamental God given nature. They disobeyed! Why? Were human beings required to sin for some supernatural cosmic purpose?

In spite of these realities, the Creator God could not tolerate disobedience. He banished them from Eden, cut off intimate association with them and condemned them to death and hell. In addition he said

"... 'I swore in my wrath, they shall never enter my rest' although his works were finished from the foundation of the world." (Hebrews 4:3)

What kind of relationship did the creator God have with his human beings? It was relationship that would tolerate no variation from absolute obedience. It was the relationship of master and slave.

If we are honest with the Biblical material we will discover the Creater God's wrath persisted through ages of time until the myth of a loving God emerged in Monistic Gnosticism and was picked up by writers of the New Testament.

Forever after obedience became the touchstone of acceptance by God. He developed programs to help them to choose the way of obedience. But it was a rough go!

All human beings persisted in the disobedient ways of their primordial ancestors. God gave up. The Creator was wrathful with all species of the human race and resolved to make a new beginning.

The Flood

He selected one family from the fragmented tribal groups as seed for his new order of human beings. The rest of the entire human race experienced his wrath as they agonized and drowned in the universal flood.

After this death dealing flood he set the survivors down on a refurbished world which augured well for a new human race. But not even one generation had passed before all the disobeying tendencies of their pre-flood ancestors reappeared.

It was becoming obvious that the Monistic God was right in declaring that all physical creation was flesh; ignorant, disobedient and evil.

The Tower of Babel

The descendents of Noah followed their primordial ancestor's lust for knowledge. They attempted to ascend to the heavens to see for themselves what was really going on in the supernatural spiritual world.

When God discovered this blatant disobedient attempt to gain the forbidden knowledge, he confused their language and made it impossible for them to cooperate in any search for supernatural spiritual knowledge or anything else. They splintered into hostile, conflicting tribal groups, whose continuing thirst for knowledge was slacked by multiple contradictory speculations: the doctrines of their religions.

This Babel experience provided a remarkable insight into the Creator God's intentions. One way to keep human beings from obtaining knowledge about spiritual reality was to keep them socially fragmented. Thus they will forever hate, quarrel and fight. They will have no time, energy or resources to construct a world of love, cooperation and peace.

Should the Creator God give up and admit defeat?

He didn't. He couldn't. It was not in the plan.

Abraham

God tried one more time to find human beings who would chose to obey him and he would make it easy for them to do so. He would make them his own, his "chosen people." They alone would be his people. He alone would be their God.

He chose Abraham and his descendents. Because of this "chosen" status they, it could be assumed, would freely chose him to be their God.

There was only one requirement:

"You shall have no other Gods before Me"

God helped them to be his exclusive people by providing social barriers: exclusive social patterns, stipulations concerning food, unique complex religious rituals and an array of special festivals. All of these were constant reminders that he alone was their God and they alone were his people.

Did this plan succeed? History has an answer!

Should the Creator God give up? Could he not recognize defeat?

No! Defeat was not in the plans which had been designed before the world was created.

All the failures of human beings had been deliberately planned before the world began. They had to be disobedient to set the stage for the crucial final act of the cosmically significant plan of salvation.

The Creator God proceeded with the crucial episodes of his plan. He incarnated his son. This also had been planned before time began.

CHAPTER 14

Incarnation and its Sequel

The Incarnation [39]

The Creator God sent his Son to this world where he became "flesh." Is this term clear? It does not refer to the physical organs of a human being! It is a condition of "ignorance of supernatural spiritual knowledge." It is this condition of "ignorance" which is "evil;" a condition established by the decree of the Monistic God and endorsed by the Creator God.

> "And the Word became flesh and dwelt among us" (John 1:14)

Is this equivalent to Paul's doctrine developed some 75 years earlier?

> "For our sake he made him to be sin who knew no sin, so that in him we might become the righteousness of God" (II Corinthians. 5:21)

The Creator God caused his son to become a full participant in the essential character of the created world; ignorance of supernatural spiritual knowledge.

Jesus of Nazareth, since he was flesh, had no knowledge of the supernatural world. He had to construct his own conception of God.[40]

However, in-spite of this physical flesh condition he was, from the Dualistic Gnostic viewpoint, still sinless for two reasons. In the first place the Creator God by his own decree had made all creation good. In the second place Jesus Christ was the Creator God's only begotten son. Therefore even a supreme God and therefore could not be evil or sin.

The crucifixion

Human beings live, do evil things and die. Christ Jesus lived, associated with sinners, was crucified with criminals and died. In addition he went to Hades. Through all this, in Dualistic Gnostic thought, he was sinless.

Three days in Hades

In the first century view of life and death, most human beings, particularly the poor and powerless simply died and that was the end. But humans of high status and power were believed to be connected to the Gods. When these humans died they went to Hades for a period of time. As the myth of Christ Jesus developed, he also experienced this additional aspect of being flesh.

However Jesus Christ was a singular exception, he was the Son of God, therefore a God and could not sin. His spirit was pure through all these experiences.

The resurrection

What kind of body did the resurrected Christ Jesus have?

> "The Patriarch David…being a prophet,…foresaw and spoke of the resurrection of the Christ, that he was not abandoned to Hades, nor did his 'flesh see corruption.'" (Acts 2:29-31)

The Creator God proved conclusively, in the incarnation, crucifixion, death, Hades and, resurrection, that the Monistic God's unilateral, arbitrary decree was not enforceable. Jesus

Christ had been flesh and endured all the consequences of that condition. He remained sinless through it all.

The Monistic God had been bested. He was proven wrong. His decree was false. Therefore he was, from the view point of Dualistic Gnosticism, not a true God. He was, in the supernatural spiritual world a false God. Could any God pronounce a more devastating rejection?

The ascension

Having won a decisive battle the son of God returned victorious to the world of the spirits. The War of the Gods was turning in favor of the Creator God.

But this was only one battle, all be it a crucial battle, in the ongoing endless War of the Gods.

Most human beings are ignorant of these super-cosmic plans

From the Gnostic point of view such "knowledge" has been deliberately withheld from human beings.

> "At that time Jesus declared, 'I thank thee Father, Lord of heaven and earth, that thou hast hidden these things from wise and understanding and revealed them to babes…and no one knows the father except the Son and any one to whom the Son chooses to reveal him.'" (Matthew 11:25-27)

But it was revealed to a few human beings in the first century CE! Only Gnostics have this knowledge!

But what, in the context of Gnostic thought, is the purpose of all these dramatic acts?

---

[39] See this word in the Glossary
[40] Ch. 5

CHAPTER 15

The Super-Cosmic Purpose

Paul of Tarsus has an explanation of the incarnation and crucifixion events based in the larger cosmic supernatural spiritual context.

> "For our sake he made him to be sin who knew no sin, so that in him we might become the righteousness of God." (II Corinthians. 5:21)

Did the Creator God do this so that human beings might become righteous? A positive answer to this question is consistent with Christian orthodoxy.

However it is the Creator God who is proven righteous

If we are honest with the fundamental thrust of this statement, in the supernatural spiritual context, it has a far different meaning. He did it so that human beings might become the evidence of the "righteousness of God!"

It is God and his righteousness that is at issue here! Paul in his letter to the Romans grappled with this issue in an extended passage:

> "...But now the righteousness of God has been manifested apart from the law...the righteousness of God through faith in Jesus Christ for all who believe...for all have sinned and fall short of the glory of God, they are justified by his grace as a gift,...This was to show God's righteousness, because in his divine

forbearance he had passed over former sins; it was to prove at the present time that he himself is righteous and that he justifies him who has faith in Jesus."(Romans 3:21-26)

The crucifixion, the central event in the plan of salvation was a demonstration that the Creator God was righteous. In what way was he right?

The Monistic God had declared the Creator God to be wrong in creating the physical universe.

Is that really true? The whole supernatural world was wondering!

The Creator God incarnated his Son in flesh. As a human being, his Son experienced all flesh characteristics and remained sinless.

The evidence is in, the verdict is clear. Flesh is not necessarily evil. Jesus Christ proved this from birth, through life, crucifixion, death, Hades, resurrection and ascension.

The Creator God, by the implementation of his plan, had proven that he was right (righteous) about creation. At the same time he had proven the Monistic God to be wrong (unrighteous).

Who in this world really cares about all this?

Maybe human beings do or should!

Human beings are justified

In Gnostic thought human beings were and are deeply involved in this on going plan. They provide evidence that their Creator God is right (righteous). Their belief and their faith in the plan of salvation, their status of being saved is the evidence.

For providing this evidence they will be rewarded, they will be justified. What is this?

Scholars, through two millennia have been confused about this word.

Some evangelists, in the 1930s did not bother with the Greek word. They used the English translation "justified" and, with this English word constructed a widely believed Christian doctrine:

"Just as if I have never sinned!"[41]

Paul made the same point in his prolix statement. Speaking about believers he says;

"...they are justified by his grace as a gift... because in his divine forbearance he had passed over former sins... This was to show God's righteousness." (Romans 3:24-26)

But he emphasizes his crucial point. God is righteous! The Creator God is right about the matter of physical creation! Human beings who believe in this formula demonstrate and prove that God is righteous. As a reward they are justified. They are effectively sinless.

By the end of six acts in the drama of the plan of salvation the Creator God has proven that He is righteous and believing human beings have become sinless. Utterly astounding.

Those sinners who believe in the reality of this drama are justified as a reward for providing evidence that the Creator

God has effectively demonstrated that flesh is not evil. They have been transformed from a condition of being sinners to the status of never having sinned.

Only Gnostics know this. This is supernatural spiritual knowledge. This is Creator God Gnosticism. This is a supernatural spiritual state. These human beings have been transformed in multiple ways. Sin will no longer be imputed to them. Although still in the "flesh," they are now spiritual or potentially spiritual in some supernatural sense, with intimate connections to the Creator God.

They get justification as a gift although they may continue to sin. Paul knew this by his own experience.

Utterly Astounding!

Any one who believes these doctrines is a Creator God Gnostic.

---

[41] I learned this from Radio Evangelists when I was a young teenager.

CHAPTER 16

The Supernatural Impact

The Creator God had proven himself to be righteous. As a side effect he had also saved believing human beings and justified them.

But the plan of salvation events, played out on our earth had profound significance in a much larger and important domain: the supernatural spiritual world.

A pseudonymous conservative Paul in his letter to Ephesians had information about these matters. In true Gnostic style he claims supernatural spiritual authority thereby raising the hope of the early Church that his revelation is authentic.

> "When you read this you can perceive my insight into the mystery of Christ which was not made known to the sons of men in other generations." (Ephesians 3:4-5a)

The mystery which had been kept secret, the wisdom of God which had been hidden from before the beginning of time, is now in the first century CE made known. The knowledge of the nature of the supernatural spiritual world, which the Creator God had deliberately withheld from human beings at the creation, was now revealed to pseudonymous Paul and his generation.

He continues his revelation:

> "...For we are not contending against flesh and blood, but against the principalities, against the powers, against the world rulers of this present darkness, against the

spiritual hosts of wickedness in heavenly places."
(Ephesians 6:12.)

We must remember that the Monistic Gods created nothing. They are the spiritual entities who had declared all creation to be "flesh," ignorant of supernatural spirituality, corrupt, destructive and evil! They are the Gods who denounced the Creator Gods as false Gods, bad Gods and other demeaning appellations.[42]

And now the Dualistic Gods, in the Gnostic view of the New Testament, have declared the Monistic Gods to be evil.

Pseudonymous Paul is a defender of the Creator God. He would see the Monistic Gods as "spiritual hosts of wickedness in heavenly places" and as "world rulers of this present darkness."

The Gods of the supernatural world are vicious name callers. Is this kind of angry exchange sufficient to perpetuate an endless war between the spirits of the supernatural world? In the context of Gnostic thought it was and is!

There are astounding consequences for human beings.

The plan of salvation was an initial battle strategy of the Creator Gods (the God of the Bible), in their eternal supernatural spiritual warfare with other Gods, the principalities and powers of darkness and wickedness in the heavenly places.

It turns out that the salvation of human beings was preliminary to and a prerequisite to the supernatural spiritual plan of the Creator Gods. Human beings had to sin in order to be saved and form the church. The Creator God needed this evidence to prove his righteousness.

Thus, in the super-cosmic context, the plan of salvation was a tool of the Creator Gods. These Gods arbitrarily manipulated human beings for their own ultimate purpose. And it was all planned before the world was created. [43]

The super cosmic purpose

As discussed in a few preceding chapters the crucifixion dealt with proving the righteousness of the Creator God.

But it also had something to do with the ignorance of "all men" and the ignorance of certain "principalities and powers in the heavenly places."

The author of Ephesians treats the subject in the early part of that letter (Ephesians Chapters 1-3) and summarizes its central thesis in the following quotation.

> "To make all men see what is the plan of the mystery hidden for ages in God who created all things, that **through the church** the manifold wisdom of God might now be made known to the principalities and powers in the heavenly places. This was according to the eternal purpose which he has realized in Christ Jesus…" (Ephesians 3:9-12)

All men were ignorant of spiritual realities. Not a great surprise! We knew that. God made human beings that way.

But now, in the late years of the first century of our era, human beings who had been saved by the crucifixion, the **church,** had supplied the evidence proving the righteousness of God and now have the opportunity to see what is really going on in the supernatural world!

In addition, a whole class of Gods had no idea what the Creator Gods were up to in their "plan of salvation." This class of Gods, the "principalities and powers in the heavenly places," were ignorant of aspects of supernatural knowledge. Utterly astounding! What was the nature of this ignorance?

It was some "wisdom of God." The Creator Gods had withheld this wisdom from human beings but also from the "principalities and powers of darkness of the heavenly regions;" the Monistic Gods and their minions!

What is this wisdom? What is this manifold mystery? What is this knowledge?

Did it have something to do with what the Creator Gods had in mind before they created the world? They had created human beings with the capacity to sin; even destined to sin and all of them, without exception, fulfilled this appointed destiny.

"...For all have sinned and fall short of the glory of God. (Romans 3:23)

And, in addition, God had decreed that sin required judgment, death and punishment. Even punishment in the furies of an eternal hell! This was the terrible ultimate condition of human beings before the plan of salvation was activated.

Such an ultimate condition is absolutely and necessarily a prerequisite to ultimate salvation. And ultimate salvation was the whole purpose of Jesus Christ coming to this world and being crucified. Only this sequence of events was sufficient to prove the righteousness of the Creator God. But it also set the stage for the other strategic plan of the Creator God in the war against the Monistic Gods.

The creation of human beings, their inevitable performance of sin, the terror of hell, the incarnation of the Son of God, the crucifixion, the resurrection and the ascension were all predetermined events in the grand design of the Creator Gods. All this required an interlude of time in the timeless eternity of the Gods and the pure spirit Gods (the Monistic Gods) knew nothing about it.

Did the Creator Gods really have all this in mind before they created time and the world? Yes! The author of Ephesians is unequivocally explicit about this matter.

But was that all? Was there more; even much more? Was there some super-cosmic reality for which all these events were necessary prerequisites?

In the context of Gnostic thought all of this was required for the activation of the plan of spiritualization and the accomplishment of its purpose. This plan is the topic of a number of following Chapters.

---

[42] Ch.8
[43] Ibid

CHAPTER 17

Spiritualization of Paul

Supernatural spiritual knowledge is inextricably linked with the performance of miracles. Miracles then, are the definitive proof of supernatural spirituality and the possession of supernatural knowledge.[44]

Paul in the promotion of his gospel argued that Jesus of Nazareth, who had been crucified almost two decades before he began his ministry, was a Christ. Certainly the best evidence to prove this point would have been references to and descriptions of miracles which Jesus of Nazareth performed.

But the Radical Paul, the authentic Paul of Tarsus, never reports a single miracle that Jesus of Nazareth did; even though the performance of miracles is the absolutely crucial proof of a spiritual connection to the supernatural world.

We must conclude that the Jesus that Paul wrote about is not Jesus of Nazareth, but an entirely different Jesus; a supernatural spiritual phenomenon which he named Jesus Christ. This Jesus Christ he met in a vision! For Saul, that vision resulted in a radical reformulation of his world view and a life changing experience. [45]

Very few human beings have visions. Those who have visions ordinarily claim unique relationships to the supernatural world or some kind of extra-sensory source. This relationship enables them to receive knowledge about unknown and unknowable realities. This is the essential character of Gnostics and their way of thinking.

Paul's writings reflect this way of thinking! As a consequence of his visionary encounter with Jesus Christ and other revelations, he became a key participant in the two plans of the Creator Gods. Did he know what he was doing?

Initially he outlined the crucial steps in the plan of salvation and called it his gospel.[46]

But Paul had a much expanded conception of his mission in this world! It was something more significant than saving human beings from the consequences of their sin.

By the time he wrote his second letter to the Corinthian church his Jesus Christ had became something vastly more intimate and significant. Jesus Christ the supernatural avatar, the emissary, the advocate, the Christ who spoke to him from an external heavenly light-now was actually in him and speaking in him. The ultimate source of wisdom and knowledge was now in him

"Christ is speaking in me." (II Corinthians. 13:3)

But there was more. Not only was Christ speaking in him. This Christ also endowed him with supernatural spiritual power. Paul could now do miracles; the definitive proof that he was intimately in contact with the supernatural world and its spiritual power He was a supernatural spiritual being although he was, in some elementary way, still in flesh and a human being.

"The signs of a true apostle were performed among you in all patience, with signs and wonders and mighty works." (II Corinthians 12:12)

Paul is writing a testimonial. But he already knew or had premonitions of this elevated spiritual condition when he wrote his first letter to the Corinthian church.

"I decided to know nothing among you except Jesus Christ and him crucified." (I Corinthians. 2:2)

Why the exception? Wasn't "Jesus Christ and him crucified" the whole gospel? What else was there? What else did he know? Why did he not tell them?

Paul admits he knows more than he is telling them. Something really important! There was more, much more! Did he know what the Creator Gods were really doing in the supernatural spiritual world and in this world?

> "But I, brethren, could not address you as spiritual men, but as men of the flesh, as babes in Christ. I fed you with milk, not solid food; for you are not ready for it and even yet you are not ready. For you are still of the flesh…Are you not merely men" (I Corinthians. 1:1-5)

Paul is writing these things to people who believed his gospel. They are people who have been "saved." But Paul says they were not spiritual men. They were "merely men" and even more devastating, they were "men of the flesh." They were still of the flesh even though they were saved and would not go to hell. They were members of his church! They were still sinners!

What is there about the flesh which makes it impossible for them to be spiritual? Where did this idea come from? How does one escape the "flesh."? How is the condition of being "merely men" to be overcome? How does one become more than a human being, more than a saved human being? How?

How does a human being become spiritual? If one becomes spiritual what are the consequences of that condition? Are there different degrees of spirituality? If there are, how does one rise in the hierarchy of "spirituality?" How does one become supernaturally spiritual.

The mystery of New Testament spirituality

Is it possible, for a normal human being, to understand this mysterious aspect of Pauline materials and other equally mystifying references to spirit and spirituality in the New Testament?

It may be possible! A framework for comprehending these doctrines is provided in the complex thought structure of Gnosticism.

The New Testament was written in a time when Gnosticism, a cross cultural philosophical-religious system of thought was popular; particularly among segments of the intellectual elites in many cultures.

Paul was an intellectual, intimately acquainted with the world views of three cultures in which he grew to maturity: the Greco-Roman-Hebrew cultural mix. In such a confusing and complex world Gnosticism provided a significant additional perspective, another world view, maybe even an alternative world view. His use of Gnostic terms and phrases and his promotion of Gnostic spirituality is incontrovertible evidence that he was very knowledgeable about Gnostic doctrine. But like all Gnostics he was a selective Gnostic.[47]

Therefore, it seems logical, if we wish to understand the New Testament we must understand this world view in addition to understanding the three cultural world views of the region which were the context of its production.[48]

Paul recalled and reported in a letter written about the mid to late 50s of the first century, another remarkable experience he had sometime after the Damascus road vision.

"I know a man in Christ who fourteen years ago was caught up to the third heaven... I know this man was caught up into Paradise." (II Corinthians. 12:2-3)

Of course Paul is writing about himself; not as an ordinary human being but as a "spiritualized" human being.

Fourteen years earlier was the time period of his retreat in the Arabian Desert and Damascus. During this period he experienced a visit to the third heaven, a rather significant spiritual experience in the context of Gnostic knowledge.

It should be noted that Mohammed, some six hundred years later, went to the seventh heaven; the heaven of perfect bliss:

"Then He completed and finished from their creation as seven heavens in two Days and He made in each heaven its affair. And We adorned the nearest heaven with light sources to be an adornment, as well as to guard. Such is the Decree of Him the All-Mighty, the All-Knower." (Quran 41:12)

Let us return to Paul. He was a man who had multiple revelations; even an:

"...abundance of Revelations..." (II Corinthians 12:7)

These successive revelations apparently provided higher levels of supernatural knowledge and wisdom. A least he had such experiences by the time he was writing his epistles.

In I Corinthians, Chapter 2&3, he elaborates on this wisdom. It is a unique kind of wisdom. It is "supernatural spiritual wisdom."

"Yet among the mature we do impart wisdom although it is not a wisdom of this age...But we do impart a secret and hidden wisdom of God…God has revealed to us through the spirit." (I Corinthians. 2:6-10)

This wisdom is not of this age. Is it wisdom of the timeless eternity? Is it wisdom of the ages created by the Creator Gods? The evidence suggests it is some of both and a lot more.

It is the kind of wisdom possessed by some of the supernatural spiritual Gods which, under certain conditions and for certain purposes, they reveal to some human beings. These become spiritualized human beings. Paul was, at least in his own mind, one of them!

This wisdom is of God. Is it knowledge about God? Is it wisdom that God has, but keeps hidden and secret. At least it is secret and hidden from "babes" But it was revealed to "us." Is Paul using the editorial "us;"? Who are these people? Paul had this "knowledge and is generous. He is prepared to share the knowledge and wisdom of God (Gnosis) with the "mature!"

But who are the mature. Are they fellow Gnostics who want to move to higher levels of spiritual knowledge. Would it ever include those who are saved but still "babes" who desperately want to become spiritual, and thereby escape the condition of being "merely men."

What about wisdom? It is revealed wisdom. And God has done this through the spirit; the Holy Spirit.

Dare we, who live in the 21st century make an observation about all of this? We live in an age where knowledge and wisdom are derived by the scientific method and not from some unknowable supernatural spiritual revelation. Are we fools? Paul thinks so!

It follows that those who want supernatural spiritual knowledge and wisdom must return to the thought structures of Gnostics who were spiritualized in the first century, or the dark ages which that century produced. Is it possible that such ideas have persisted into the 21st century? Is it possible that such wisdom guides dominant ideologies of the powerful in our society?

But there still might be some people who want such knowledge and wisdom and think in first century categories and pray to experience such spiritual gifts. What of them?

Supernatural spirituality is God's gift to give. Does he give it to any one who wants this kind of spirituality? Apparently the Creator God chooses those who receive this gift. Paul believed he was one of the chosen!

"… we have received…the spirit which is from God that we might understand the gifts bestowed upon us." (I Corinthians. 2: 12)

Paul and other spiritual people had this gift. They were superior to all others. So superior in fact, that utter arrogance, consummate hubris, is a mark of the advanced spiritual man.

"The spiritual man judges all things, but is to be judged by no one." (I Corinthians 2:15)

Is this another incarnation? Paul's Jesus Christ is much more than an ordinary emissary from the supernatural world; he is the Son of God. This ultimate spiritual being was not only speaking in Paul, but also worked in him to perform miracles; the ultimate proof of spirituality and apparently also proof of being a true disciple.

"The signs of a true disciple were performed among you in all patience, with signs and wonders and mighty works." (II Corinthians. 12: 12)

For Paul the disciples of Jesus of Nazareth were not true disciples. They did no miracles. Therefore they were not spiritual. Were they false disciples?

And Paul was also above sin.

---

[44] Refer to Chapter 8 See also Appendix D

[45] Snider Howard M. – Jesus or Christ, Infinity Press, Conshohoken, Pa. 2009

[46] Refer to Chapter 8

[47] Ibid

[48] Consult my three earlier books

CHAPTER 18

Supernatural Spirituality and Sin

Although Paul was a Creation God Gnostic he adopted the "flesh" aspect of Monistic, Ultimate Unity Gnosticism. He made it a central feature of his plan of salvation gospel. In this kind of theology human beings are flesh. For human beings flesh and sin are inseparable. For Paul, sin was a crucial issue. Even to undo the consequences of that condition, required, in the myth he constructed, the crucifixion of the most precious thing in God's universe, God's only son. This complex doctrine was Paul's gospel and the formative factor in the literature of the New Testament.

If we read the Pauline materials, both authentic and pseudonymous, we find their words and phrases betray their commitment to Gnostic doctrines. Paul was, in general a Dualistic Gnostic. He knows he is not an illusion; he is a human being, a part of creation. He is flesh. His God was the Creator God!

The doctrine of free will is an underlying assumption in the story of the fall and also in some versions of the atonement doctrine which Paul promoted in his Gospel. He could not escape the fact that his good God had created human beings with the capacity and an inescapable tendency to sin.

Paul has a major problem.

He has supernatural spiritual knowledge. He also has been possessed by God's spirit, the Holy Spirit. He has become a spiritual being, in fact a supernatural spiritual being. It follows that he should be good like his God.

Why does he yet sin? A profound conundrum!

> "I know that nothing good dwells within me, that is, in
> my flesh…I do not do the good I want, but the evil that I
> do not want is what I do. Now if I do what I do not
> want, it is no longer I who do it, but sin that dwells
> within me." (Romans 7:15-20)

> "…with my flesh I serve the law of sin. (Romans 7:23)

Paul in his world view is aware he is flesh and he knows that
sin is what the flesh does. But the Creator God made him and
made him flesh. Who then is really responsible for Paul's
behavior? Is it Paul or is it God? He claims he is not
responsible. He blames it on flesh which he identifies as the
"law of sin." A Monistic Gnostic would surely approve of
this conclusion.

However he knows, in his Creator God Gnostic perspective,
he is now a supernatural spiritual being and in this
transformed reality he is beyond the consequences of
creation. Flesh and sin are irrelevant and he is not
responsible for either one.

According to Luke, Paul and other believers who have been
selected, spiritualized and initiated into esoteric supernatural
spiritual knowledge will ultimately live an eternal life.

> "…and as many as were ordained to eternal life
> believed" (Acts 13:48)

Paul's problem with his own doctrine

Paul, however, had problems with some aspects of his own
Gnostic doctrine. He had a member in the Corinthian church

who believed that he had advanced in spiritual enlightenment to the point where matters of the flesh were totally irrelevant.

> "...there is immorality among you...a man who is living with his father's wife. And you are arrogant!" (I Corinthians 5:1-2.)

Other members in that congregation seemed to tolerate this behavior. Were they sympathetic with this Monistic Gnostic viewpoint?

These are a few examples which demonstrate a fundamental human process. Human beings select, from their social environment, those ideas which support their purposes and their belief system. Paul and his followers, in spite of their supernatural spiritual self perceptions, were human beings in this respect.

Paul of Tarsus concluded his ministry in Asia Minor and Greece about 65 CE. He had been arrested by Roman authorities, made an appeal to Emperor Nero and was sent to Rome. According to some traditions he spent his last years as a member of the Jewish Diaspora in that city. In other traditions he was executed in Rome. He wrote nothing more.

Paul – the subject of myth creation

His concepts of supernatural spirituality, his emphasis on spiritual power and supernatural spiritual knowledge mark him as a selective Dualistic Gnostic. He laid the foundation for the more extensive Christian Gnostic doctrines which appear in later writings in the New Testament.

Paul himself became the subject of myths. Some of these appear in the pseudo-Pauline materials, and a document by Luke, The Acts of the Apostles provide many of these.

Luke, writing in the last decade of the first century, finally reports for the first time the myths of Paul's first and last visions.

Two myths, reported more than sixty years after the alleged events, refer to Saul's first vision and its immediate sequel.

> "Now as he was going along and approaching Damascus, suddenly a light from heaven flashed around him. He fell to the ground and heard a voice saying to him, 'Saul, Saul, why do you persecute me?' He asked, 'Who are you, Lord?' The reply came, 'I am Jesus, whom you are persecuting.'" (Acts 9:3-5)

> "Brother Saul, the Lord Jesus, who appeared to you on your way here, has sent me so that you may regain your sight and be filled with the Holy Spirit." (Acts:9:17.)

The last myths, developed in the thirty years after Paul went to Rome, are reported by Luke.

> "The following night the Lord stood by him and said 'take courage, for as you have testified about me at Jerusalem, so you must bear witness also in Rome.'" (Acts 23:11)

On the way he had an opportunity in Malta.

> "...a viper came out of the fire...and fastened on his hand...He however shook off the viper...they ...expected him to fall down dead but...saw no misfortune come to him, they changed their minds and said that he was a God." (Acts 28:4-6)

Paul finally, more than fifty years after he had persecuted Jesus followers, became known as a supernatural being, even something of a God.

CHAPTER 19

Followers Spiritualized

The disciples of Jesus of Nazareth were human beings. They could do no miracles. Because of this deficiency Paul asserted that they were not true disciples!

The Gospels of Mark and Matthew, the pseudonymous Pauline materials, the work of Luke and the gospel of John all appeared after Paul had gone to Rome. By this time according to these documents Paul, followers of Paul, disciples of Jesus, other followers of Jesus and finally Jesus himself were reported as doing miracles. How is this possible?

There were no journalists, historians or recording devices present at any of the purported events included in these documents. In spite of these indisputable realities the documents written by Matthew, Mark, Luke and John are laced with quotations credited to Paul, the apostles, other followers of Jesus and Jesus himself.

We know it was an era of amazing facility in oral communication. But it beggars the imagination to believe that, after many generations of story telling, these materials reflect accurate or dependable information about any of the events or statements reported.

However, whether they have any historical validity or not is irrelevant. They are the stories, the world views of the Christian church in the late first and early second centuries CE. They have the earmarks of crystallized Gnostic mythology. If we dare to be honest with the New Testament we must see it in this light.

118

Given this reality they are remarkably informative. They inform us about the world views of the cultures which produced Christianity and the early years of the Christian Church.

Do they have any relevance for us in our scientific age?

The disciples who had actually companied with Jesus of Nazareth while he was alive, had heard him talk about the way his God wanted human beings to live in this world; the way of love. They believed in the value of this revolutionary way of living. They wanted a change in the social life of their world; a change in the way humans related to one another.

But by the end of the century that story had been turned upside down. By then Jesus, obviously the Jesus Christ of Paul's vision, promised them the Holy Spirit and gave them a task.

"...for John baptized with water but before many days you will be baptized by the Holy Spirit; and you shall be witnesses to the end of the earth. (Acts 1:8)

All the writers mentioned above believed that promoting Paul's doctrines and doing supernatural spiritual things like miracles were more important than changing social life in this world.

According to a sequel to that story, also written sixty years after the purported event, it happened:

"When the day of Pentecost had fully come, they were all together in one place. And suddenly a sound came from heaven like the rush of a mighty wind... And they were all filled with the Holy Spirit and began to speak in other tongues..." (Acts 2:1-5)

The disciples, apparently all of them, were suddenly, miraculously, multi-lingual; positive proof that they had connections to the supernatural spirits.

By the end of the century, instead of getting the kingdom of God on earth (the social revolution which Jesus of Nazareth has promised} they, according to the developed myth, got a supernatural commission to promote the spiritualization of human beings.

These supernaturally spiritualized people were empowered to do miracles and were being prepared for a transition to the supernatural world after death. As supernatural spiritual beings they would not corrupt themselves with human social problems. Social conditions in this world would be concerns of the flesh. As spiritual beings they were beyond such earthly matters. They would do miracles.

The New Testament is massive internal evidence that the Gnostic doctrine of spiritualization and miracles are inextricably intertwined.

More examples follow.

Peter and John became examples of miracle working disciples. They demonstrated their special relationship with the supernatural world.

"...a man lame from birth...laid daily... to ask alms of those who entered the temple... And Peter directed his gaze at him, with John, and ...Peter said to him" I have no silver or gold , but I give you what I have; in the name of 'Jesus Christ' of Nazareth, walk...and immediately his feet and ankles were made strong." (Acts 3:3-7)

By the end of the first century Jesus of Nazareth had been completely absorbed into Paul's vision of Jesus Christ. Luke even combines together a name "Jesus Christ of Nazareth;" an absolute contradiction!

"Jesus of Nazareth's" understanding of his God's will, loving, redemptive, human social relations in this world, had been displaced by supernatural relationships and individualistic miracles.

> "Now many signs and wonders were done among the people through the apostles acts…so that they even carried out the sick into the streets, and laid them on cots and mats, in order that Peter's shadow might fall on some of them as he came by. A great number of people would also gather from the towns around Jerusalem, bringing the sick and those tormented by unclean spirits, and they were all cured." (Acts 5:12-16)

By he end of the first century, Peter even had the power of life and death. Ananias and his wife Sapphira had lied about a business deal and apparently defrauded the church. Peter confronted them. They both fell down dead. (Acts 5:1-11)

> "Let all the house of Israel, therefore know assuredly that God has made him Lord and Christ, this Jesus whom you have crucified. …And Peter said to them, 'repent, and be baptized everyone of you, in the name of Jesus Christ for the forgiveness of your sin; and you shall receive the gift of the Holy Spirit. For the promise is to you and to your children and to all that are far off, every one whom the Lord our God calls to him.'" (Acts 2:36-39)

But only those "whom the Lord our God calls to him!"

And all of these miracles were done, according to Luke, a decade or more before Saul had his "Damascus Road" vision, encountered the supernatural Christ and received the Holy Spirit.

How is it possible that Peter can do anything in the name of "Jesus Christ." "Jesus Christ," Saul's mental construct, did not yet exist.

Paul, a contemporary of these alleged events, knew nothing about such miracles by the disciples. He even rejects any notion that the disciples could do miracles.

Spiritualization of early followers of Jesus

While Saul was persecuting the followers of Jesus of Nazareth, and certainly before he had his Damascus road vision, some common followers of Jesus, according to Luke, performed miracles. Philip is an example.

> "...Saul laid waste the church, and entering house after house, he dragged off men and women and committed them to prison. Now those who were scattered about went preaching the word. Philip went down to the city of Samaria and proclaimed to them 'Christ.' The multitudes with one accord gave heed to what was said by Philip, when they heard him and saw the signs which he did. For unclean spirits came out of many who were possessed; crying with a loud voice, and many who were paralyzed or lame were healed." (Acts 8:3-7)

Philip "proclaimed to them Christ." What "Christ" is this? Saul was still persecuting the followers of Jesus.

Spiritualization of Aliens

These Samaritans, these non-Jews, had heard the word of God. Some believed and were baptized to demonstrate their faith. The plan of salvation had been activated for them. They had been "saved." But they had not been "spiritualized."

> "Now when the apostles at Jerusalem heard that Samaria had received the word of God, they sent to them Peter and John, who came down and prayed for them that they might receive the Holy Spirit; for...they had only been baptized in the name of the Lord Jesus. Then they laid their hands on them and they received the Holy Spirit." (Acts 8:14-17)

For Luke, being "spiritualized" was something vastly more significant than being "saved." It would have two remarkable consequences. It would enable them to do miracles and, according to the pseudonymous Pauls' writing twenty-five years earlier, would initiate them into the esoteric knowledge of the world of supernatural spirits. This kind of knowledge is the most fundamental principle of Gnosticism.

These things, according to Luke, were being done by the very people who Saul had been persecuting. Yet after his "conversion" Saul (Paul) never references these events, even though the ability of these alien peoples to do miracles would be the most powerful proofs of his "divinity of Jesus" doctrine! Why did he never mention these people or any of their miracles?

Luke, a Greek, is writing about events, which for him had occurred in the alien cultures of Palestine and Samaria. What were the sources available to Luke as he wrote these stories more than sixty years after they ostensibly occurred? Paul had provided not a hint, even by the late sixties.

By the end of the first century "spiritualized Christianity" was exclusively concerned about the supernatural world. Jesus of Nazareth and his loving way of living had disappeared.

CHAPTER 20

Jesus of Nazareth: Spiritualized

Central to the formulation of the Christian Icons mentioned in Appendix E are the processes of progressive "supernatural spiritualization." This occurred in a major way, in the century after the crucifixion of Jesus of Nazareth. During this period, according to the New Testament, Paul of Tarsus and many of his followers became "supernaturally spiritualized," as described in preceding chapters.

It is now time to consider the myths about the spiritualization of Jesus of Nazareth. When and how did he become a supernatural spiritual being?

Christian myths in Matthew, Mark and Luke

By the eight decade CE Matthew and Mark were writing their gospels. Some oral stories were available providing various "spiritualization" myths. Some myths suggest that Jesus of Nazareth was a supernatural being from the very beginning.

> "…that which is conceived in her is of the Holy Spirit," (Matthew 1:20b)

The Holy Spirit, one of the three major spirits in later triune Christianity, fathered Jesus. Consequently, from this view point, Jesus was a God-Man, destined to do heroic things including miracles.

Also by this time there was a complex of myths relating to the supernatural celebration of the birth of Jesus. The heavenly abode of spirits and spirits themselves burst forth with celebrations, spectacular illuminations and celestial movements:

> "...there were shepherds...an Angel of the Lord appeared to them and the glory of the Lord shone around them..." (Luke 2:8-9)

> "And suddenly there was with the angel a multitude of the heavenly host praising God and saying, 'Glory to God'..." (Luke 2:13-14a)

> "Wise men came from the East....for we have seen his star in the East." (Matthew 2:1-2)

> "The star which they had seen in the East went before them."(Matthew 2:9)

Who is this God-Man that can excite spiritual beings of the supernatural world?"

Paul never mentions any of these marvelous events! They would surely have been the most spectacular proofs of the supernatural origins of Jesus.

Mark, probably the earliest of the Gospels, knows nothing about the birth of Jesus. But he knows the story about the spiritualization of Jesus which occurred in adulthood.

> "...Jesus was baptized...when he came out of the water... the heavens opened and the spirit descended upon him like a dove; and a voice came from heaven, 'Thou art my beloved Son...' (Mark 1:9-11)

He is a son of heaven. He is the son of a voice! But what voice? Was it the voice of Moses burning bush?

By the time Matthew is writing, Jesus is a God-man, and even more. He is a supernatural spiritual being on two counts: supernatural conception and supernatural baptism. This should be convincing evidence to any myth believer.

But there is more. Jesus is Lord of the spiritual world; even the Lord of his Father's enemies.

The Devil, a spirit from the world of the spirits, knows Jesus is the son of God.

> "And the tempter came to him and said 'If you are the Son of God cast yourself down'...and Jesus said 'you shall not tempt the Lord your God.'" (Matthew 4:5-7)

God! Yes, we knew that! But, "**Lord**?" Jesus proclaimed himself to be the ultimate authority and power of the universe!

And Jesus used his authority and power.

> "...The devil...showed him all the kingdoms of the world...'All these I will give you'...Jesus said to him, 'Be gone Satan!'" (Matthew 4:7-10)

> "...two demoniacs meet him ...and the demons begged him, 'If you cast us out, send us away into the herd of swine'. And he said to them 'Go.' So they came out from him and went into the swine." (Matthew 8:28-32)

Where is the Monistic God in all of this? Were the devils his emissaries on Earth? Was this another skirmish in the battle of the Gods in which the Monistic Gods and their minions was bested?

The evidence from these materials is conclusive. By the end of the first century early Christians were worshipping the powerful supernatural spiritual authority; the Lord Jesus Christ.

Luke in the 10th decade CE uses this kind of terminology as the fundamental character of Jesus.

The Spiritualization of Jesus: John's view

By the second century a writer using the name John the Baptist, repeats the myth which appeared in all the Gospels before his.

"I saw the spirit descend as a dove from heaven, and it remained on him…this is he who baptizes with the Holy Spirit…this is the Son of God." (John 1:33-34)

This event, reported in the last Gospel to be incorporated in the New Testament is remarkable in a number of ways.

Before this event, according to John, Jesus of Nazareth was a human being; an astounding deviation from the birth stories of some earlier writings.

Jesus of Nazareth was, for this John, endowed with a spirit from the supernatural world when he was a mature adult. This spirit was not just any spirit, of which there were many, who occasionally commuted between heaven and earth. This was the Holy Spirit. This is the very Spirit of God. This is ultimate spirituality and it happened to a human being; Jesus of Nazareth!

In all the Gospels the spirit descended as a dove. This phrase has inspired considerable Christian art. The dove is a bird which inhabits the region between heaven and earth. It, in a figurative way, can approach and touch both domains and is thus a symbol of spiritual activity. But why a lowly dove rather than a powerful eagle?

Is it because a dove has a voice and is more often heard than seen?

The spirits, the Gods of Greco-Roman culture, came to earth and arbitrarily interacted with human beings. But the humans rarely knew what had happened until after the event and then only if they experienced some marvelous misfortune or unusual good fortune.

The Gods of Abram and Moses spoke but were not seen. Saul of Tarsus heard a voice speaking in the context of a blinding light, but saw nothing.

But when the supernatural spirit comes to Jesus; John sees! He sees, in symbolic form, the ultimate power of the spiritual and physical worlds enter a human being. Only a Gnostic; a spiritualized human being could recognize this reality.

And John already had this knowledge before the event occurred.

> "...but *he who sent me* to baptize with water said to me, 'He on whom you see the spirit descend and remain, this is he who baptizes with the Holy Spirit.'"(John.1:32-33)

Who sent him? Obviously it was some supernatural spirit who was knowledgeable about this baptismal plan. John had supernatural knowledge!

The progression of spiritualization reported in these myths are remarkable examples of the accretions and variations which occur in the storytelling activity of oral cultures. Multitudes of such myths have controlled the life of millions of people through two millennia!

Chapter 21

John, Spirituality and Gnosticism

John, writing his gospel sometime in the first third of the second century, is partial to Dualistic Gnosticism.

The Monistic Gods of the heavens had created nothing. From their viewpoint all creation had been produced, by inferior demi-Gods. Therefore the physical universe and everything in it was devoid of true spiritual knowledge. It was "flesh," therefore evil, degenerate and destructive.[49]

John rejects this basic doctrine of Monistic Gnosticism. The prologue to his Gospel is a remarkably clear statement of the most crucial doctrine of Dualistic Gnosticism. (John 1:1-18)

He points out that "Logos" {"The Word?" "Truth?" "Jesus Christ?" "God?") was present at and performed the Creation of time and the physical universe.

"In the beginning was the word, and the word was with God and the word was God." (Jn.1:1)

"All things were made through him…" (Jn.1:3)

"…the world was made through him," (Jn.1:10)

John is obviously reacting against the Monistic Gnosticism which troubled proto-orthodox bishops of the early church in the second century. He endorses the Genesis account and agrees that creation was "good."

In addition he endows the Creator God and his son with all the positive characteristics which had been claimed by the

Monistic God. Light, life, enlightenment, grace and truth are the essential characteristics of Monistic Gnostic spirituality. John is obviously a selective Gnostic. He attributes all these characteristics to his Creator Gods.

"...in him was life and the life was the light of men."... (Jn.1:4)

"The true light that enlightens every man..." (John 1:9)

"...full of grace and truth. (John 1:14)

And then John makes one of the most astounding statements in the New Testament if not in the whole Bible:

"And the Word became "flesh" and dwelt among us... (John 1:14)

John is writing a hundred years after the crucifixion. This event, in the context of Dualistic Gnosticism, had proven that "flesh" was not evil. John is emphasizing the verdict of the crucifixion in Dualistic Gnostic terms.

The evidence suggests that a powerful segment of early Christianity were Dualistic Gnostics. The proto-orthodox churches were worshipping the Lord Jesus Christ. They were not worshipping, much less following, Jesus of Nazareth.

Jesus or Lord Jesus Christ

This is not surprising. Paul, many years earlier, had promoted Jesus as a Christ, Lord and God. By the time the writers of the gospels had done their work during the next one hundred years, such terminology was common in the Christian literature. One must also conclude that such terminology was common in the conversation of illiterate Christians.

The name Jesus is used extensively in most of the Gospels. Is this the same "Jesus" who proclaimed the beatitudes? Is it really possible?

"Blessed are the poor in spirit…" (Matthew 5:3- 11)

Blessed are those who have specific behavioral characteristics. They mourn, are poor in spirit, meek, merciful, pure in heart and peacemakers. They are persecuted and reviled. These behavioral characteristics are antithetical to the very essence of authority and power of a Lord.

Jesus of Nazareth cared about the poor, the powerless and the marginal masses. He had nothing in common with the powerful authoritarian "Lord Jesus Christ" of Paul's gospel.

Is there simply a profound, inexplicable contradiction in all of this material or is it a description of reality from a Dualistic Gnostic point of view?

"…He raised him from the dead and made him sit at his right hand in the heavenly places, far above all rule and authority and power and dominion…not only in this age but that which is to come. (Ephesians 1:20-21)

At any rate the gospel of Paul, by the second century, had trumped the gospel of Jesus of Nazareth. The writer of the gospel of John provides the capstone argument that the doctrines developed by Paul had became encapsulated in Dualistic Gnosticism, the central mythology of the New Testament and the early Church.

---

[49] See – Ch 8

CHAPTER 22

The Purpose of Spiritualization

The conservative and reactionary Pauls had knowledge of the supernatural world. They knew the Monistic God had decreed that non-spirit realities were "flesh." Avatars, demiurges and other kinds of spirits emanated from the Monistic God. Some of these spirits conspired to create a physical universe and its human beings and became known as Creator Gods or Dualistic Gods.

These Monistic and Dualistic supernatural spiritual powers have engaged in competition and conflict since the beginning of time. In this context they have recruited human beings to fight their battles in the earthly theatre of their war. These humans must become spirits compatible with the spirits of the supernatural world to be effective in this task. They have to go through the processes of spiritualization.

The human beings who have been saved by the plan of salvation are eligible to be in the pool of raw recruits to be trained for the War of the Gods. The plan of spiritualization is the training experience which includes the acquisition of extensive esoteric knowledge.

> "…and to make all men see what is the plan of the mystery hidden for ages, who created all things; that through the church the manifold wisdom of God, might be known to the principalities and powers in the heavenly places. This was according to the eternal purpose which he has realized in Christ Jesus." (Ephesians 3:9-11)

The church which Paul created with his gospel was a tool to convey this manifold wisdom. It was the instrument to expose the supernatural mysteries. The pseudonymous Pauls are very explicit about this matter.

The Ultimate Unity, the Monistic God, had decreed that any created thing was flesh, thereby ignorant of supernatural spiritual knowledge and consequently evil and corrupt.

Even many who believed Paul's gospel were "mere men", "babes" and lacking "maturity." They were not spiritualized and may even have lacked the characteristics required for spiritualization.

The Creator Gods made human beings and declared that all creation was good. But like the Monistic God, they withheld knowledge of the supernatural spiritual world. In the Monistic Gnostic view of things this condition is the essence of "flesh;" and human beings were therefore evil. They also sin.

Do these conditions serve the ultimate purposes of the Creator Gods in their war with the Monistic Gods? What were the Creator Gods trying to do by withholding knowledge of the supernatural world from their crowning creation? What were they trying to do with their plan of salvation and their plan of spiritualization?

Are the Creator Gods getting back at the Monistic Gods in some eternal spiritual way; some supra-cosmic way? Are the Creator Gods undoing what the Monistic Gods had done with their decree? Was this the point of contention between the Gods? Was it the issue in their warfare?

What in the world is going on?

More importantly, what in the heavenly places is going on?

Christ Jesus is the key to it all! But Paul, in creating the church based on the doctrines of his gospel, turned the key.

His gospel revealed God's plan to save human beings from evil and the consequences of sin. But, according to the documents of the pseudonymous Pauls it had a purpose grounded in the very nature of the supernatural spiritual world; the conflicts between the spirits of that heavenly realm. The problem between the Gods continues.

The Creator Gods need help. He is looking for recruits in this world and has the power to turn qualified human beings into spirits; supernatural spiritual beings. This is a function, probably the crucial function, of the Holy Spirit.

The objective of spiritualization is the transformation of human beings into spiritual beings. These spiritualized human beings then learn spiritual disciplines and thereby become trained soldiers in the army of the Creator Gods.

> "...For we are not contending against flesh and blood, but against the principalities, against the powers, against the world rulers of this present darkness, against the spiritual hosts of wickedness in the heavenly places." (Ephesians 6:12)

Spiritualized Christians in the 21st century know this. The battle is raging!

> "Put on the whole armor of God that you may be able to stand against the wiles of the devil." (Ephesians 6:11)

Christians, in the final analysis, are not only struggling against their tendencies to sin. They are actually training to be soldiers in the War of the Gods. A commitment to such training is an objective of Christians seeking advancement in supernatural spiritual qualities.

A pseudonymous Paul laid the foundation for such resolve 2,000 years ago. For two millennia serious followers of the doctrines of the Bible have made a variety of interpretations of the above quotations.

Among these are at least three ways in which Christians understand their role as soldiers in this conflict.

1) Some Christians see their role as promoting the qualities of life demonstrated by Jesus of Nazareth. Jesus was partial toward the poor and marginal in his society. Therefore he and his God were on the side of the poor. The "world rulers of this present darkness," supported by the rich and powerful humans, represent the false Gods. These powers are obviously enemies of the Creator God.

For the followers of Jesus this is true in the 21st century. Those who recognize these realities work for social change. They are committed to justice and equality for all people. An example of such a follower of Jesus is Franklin Raber. While a college student in the early 1920s he composed words for a song which his quartet often sang. Stanzas 2 and 3 make a significant Gnostic point.

"Since I have a part in God's plan divine, I am preparing, preparing. In God's army I am resolved to serve all time. So I'm preparing, preparing."

"That God may use me as to him seems right, I am preparing, preparing. I know not where I shall stand in the fight. But I'm preparing, preparing." [50]

2) Other Christians, probably the majority in our society, also see the conflict in the earthly domain of this universe but think in nationalistic terms. They divide the nations of the world into two categories: the good and the evil. Their own nation, they believe, is always on the side of God.

Enemy nations are on the side of the devil and must be controlled or destroyed by any means possible. Hence super-patriotism and participation in war are the highest forms of service to God. [51]

3) To other supernaturally spiritualized Christians this world is of little importance. They have vastly more important things to do; things that are supernaturally spiritual in their dimensions.

> "If you have been raised with Christ, seek the things that are above…Set your minds on things that are above, not on things that are on earth."(Colossians 3:1-3)

Social conditions of oppression, injustice, extreme stratification and even slavery are acceptable in this world.

> "Slaves, obey in everything those who are your earthly masters…" (Colossians3:22; Ephesians 6:5)

Their commission and task in this world has a single focus.

> "…to make known …the glory of this mystery, which is Christ in you." (Colossians 1:27).

Paul, during the few years of his ministry, worked to engage his saved followers in the spiritualization process so they might have the knowledge of these supernatural realties.

To summarize again; Paul preached his Gospel. Those who believed were saved from the wrath of the Creator God. But this was only a prerequisite to the later processes of spiritualization which is obviously more important.

> "…to have all the riches of assured understanding and knowledge of God's mystery, of Christ in whom are

138

hidden all the treasures of wisdom and knowledge."
(Colossians. 2:2-3).

Hidden wisdom and knowledge, esoteric knowledge; these
are the crucial doctrines of Dualistic Gnosticism.

"...according to the eternal purpose which he has
realized in Christ Jesus..."(Ephesians 3:9-12)

Although the radical Paul may not have written the letters to
the Ephesians or Colossians his followers had learned his
doctrines well:

"Howbeit we speak wisdom among them that are
perfect...the wisdom of God in a mystery, even the
hidden wisdom, which God ordained before the world
unto our glory."(I Corinthians 2:6)

But this wisdom is not available to everyone, even to those
who believe in the sacrifice at Calvary. This wisdom which
existed before the world began is knowledge accessible to
humans who truly love God and are supernaturally spiritual.
They are trained warriors for the Dualistic God.

By the end of the first century when Luke was writing, many
human beings had been recruited. They had been endowed
with the Holy Spirit. Among these, in a time sequence, as the
myths developed were Paul and some of his church
members, then disciples of Jesus and their followers and
finally Jesus of Nazareth himself.

---

[50] Raber, Merrill and Boots – History of the Christian Raber Family;
Graphic Images, Newton Ks 2004
[51] Constantinian Christianity. See Appendix F

CHAPTER 23

The Ultimate Reward

When spiritualized human beings have served their lifetime term of service in the earthly theatre of the War of the Gods, unimaginable rewards prepared by God await them. Radical Paul is privy to the glorious nature of these rewards.

"Eye hath not seen, nor ear heard, neither have entered into the heart of man the things which God hath prepared for them that love him. (I Corinthians. 2:9)

"For our citizenship is in heaven, from which also we eagerly wait for a Savior, the Lord Jesus Christ; who will transform the body of our humble state into conformity with the body of His glory, by the exertion of the power that He has even to subject all things to Himself." (Philippians 3:20-21 NASB)

"So also is the resurrection of the dead. It is sown a perishable body, it is raised an imperishable body; it is sown in dishonor, it is raised in glory; it is sown in weakness, it is raised in power; it is sown a natural body, it is raised a spiritual body. If there is a natural body, there is also a spiritual body." (I Corinthians.15:42-44 NASB)

"For we know that if the earthly tent we live in is destroyed, we have a building from God, a house not made with hands, eternal in the heavens." (II Cor.5:1)

And all of this was designed before the world began.

"…God ordained before the world unto our glory." (I Corinthians 2:6)

None of this was accidental. It was all planned before time was created. Human beings are side effect beneficiaries of the Creator God's plans which were made before the world was made.

The revelation of wisdom: esoteric, mysterious, sacred, secret knowledge are the crucial characteristics of Gnosticism. Aspects of this knowledge were the philosophical constructs of some thinkers of the Near East during the centuries surrounding the period in which the New Testament was written. Could any intellectual of the time be unaware of such compelling ideas?

The writers of the New Testament tapped into this system of thought in an attempt to make sense of the crucifixion. Paul was an intellectual. He struggled to make sense of these ideas in the cultural and intellectual context in which he lived. Did he succeed?

In this system of thought, human beings who become supernaturally spiritual will be participants in the domain of the Gods forever!

Spiritualized church members by the eighth decade of the first century CE, according to Ephesians, were warriors in the earthly theatre of the war of the Gods. Christians, since they have all this spiritual knowledge, are empowered to demonstrate and make known the manifold wisdom of God to all men. That seems reasonable.

But, according to the New Testament, spiritualized human beings had knowledge and wisdom even beyond that possessed by a class of Gods who occupied the heavenly places.

This is an astounding piece of knowledge.

CHAPTER 24

Features of Christian Orthodoxy

My book **Two Gospels** (2011) attempted to differentiate the gospel of Jesus of Nazareth and the gospel of Paul of Tarsus.

The essence of Paul's Gospel was his conversion of the crucified Jesus of Nazareth into a supernatural being. This was a mental construct, which he called "Jesus Christ" or "Christ Jesus." In Paul's view this "Jesus Christ" was an emissary from the supernatural world; a representative of God, even the "only begotten" son of the God who had created the physical universe.

This God-Man, according to Paul, was crucified with the consent, even the deliberate plan of his father. In the context of Christian orthodoxy this God-Man, in his crucifixion, was a sacrifice sufficient to atone for or to undo the consequences of all the sins of the human race. Or, in a more Biblical interpretation, the crucifixion terminated the "wrath of God," which had been his relationship with his disobedient human beings for all the ages of the Old Testament.

But this plan, if it was to accomplish these purposes, required human beings to respond in two ways. It required human beings to believe in the validity of the plan and have faith that it would work. If they believed and had faith they would be saved from the consequences of their sin.

And there was more to the plan. Or more realistically, a second plan!

Jesus Christ's father, the Creator God, restored him to life. This resurrection presaged more resurrections. In fact it would enable human beings to be resurrected as supernatural spiritual beings even while still living in this world. Ultimately those who were both saved and spiritualized would be accommodated with a permanent abode in the heavens, in the presence of God and his son Jesus Christ for eternity.

The Gospel of Paul, which he preached throughout Asia Minor and South East Europe, was based on this formula: But its efficacy depended on an intellectual commitment to the supernatural dimensions of each part of the formula. Communities of individuals who believed, who had faith, in the first component of this formula were the Churches to whom he wrote his epistles.

The members of these churches then had the opportunity to become spiritualized human beings. They could receive Gnosis. But this required additional belief and faith.

What is belief?
What is faith?

Belief and Faith

Pistis and **Pisteuo** are two Greek words which occur more than 500 times in the Greek New Testament. They are variously translated in English.

They are crucial to understanding the contradictions and confusions of the New Testament and Christianity in its variations during the last two millennia. Many scholars have studied these words and their work has promoted a range of interpretations.

Pistis is a noun, commonly translated as "belief" or "faith." Pisteuo (Pistevo) is a verb commonly translated as "belief" or "believing."

What do these words mean to the average Christian? Many people who are asked to define "faith" commonly reply "belief." And conversely when they are asked to define belief they reply "faith." These terms, for the average Christian, are apparently interchangeable.

But theologians and language experts have not done much better.

Pistis (*pis'-tis*) is translated in Strong's Bible Dictionary in various ways:

> "persuasion, i.e. credence; moral conviction (of religious truth, or the truthfulness of God or a religious teacher), especially reliance upon Christ for salvation; abstractly, constancy in such profession; by extension, the system of religious (Gospel) truth itself:-assurance, belief, believe, faith, fidelity." (Strong's Bible Dictionary. Item 4102)

And a 1999 definition.

> "Conviction of the truth of anything, belief,…a conviction or belief respecting man's relationship to God and divine things, generally with the included idea of trust and holy fervor born of faith and joined with it – relating to God."(Thayer and Smith. "Greek Lexicon." TheNASNewTestamentGreekLexicon)(www.biblestudy tools.com/lexicons/greek/nas/pistis.html)

Pisteuo (Pistevo)

> "pisteuo –(*pist-yoo'-o*) – to have faith (in, upon, or with respect to, a person or thing), i.e. credit; by implication, to entrust (especially one's spiritual well-being to Christ):- believe, commit (to trust, put in trust with)." (www.biblestudytools.com/lexicons/greek/nas/pistis.html)

144

Some Greek Orthodox scholars define and apply "pistis" and "pistevo" to religion as stated by Irene Alexandrau. (Praxis Greek Word Study. Posting date 14 September, 2006, (http://www.helleniccomserve.com/wordstudy.html)

Pistis (noun) means:

> "persuasion, i.e., credence; moral conviction (of religious truth, or the truthfulness of God or a religious teacher), especially reliance upon Christ for salvation; the system of religious (Gospel) truth itself; assurance, belief, believe, faith."

Pistevo (verb) means:

> "to have faith (in, upon, or with respect to, a person or thing), i.e. credit; by implication, to entrust, (especially one's spiritual well-being to Christ) believe, commit, (to trust), put trust in."

Obviously the confusion of terms and meanings in these definitions are just as circular as the common definitions of most Christians.

Some scholars take seriously the distinction between noun and verb. In my seminary days Dr. Howard Charles left me with an understanding of these Greek terms.

"Pistis," the noun, is adequately translated as either "faith" or "belief." These terms refer to intellectual constructs, the foundational system of thought, the ideology, the myth, the world view relative to the relationship of human beings to the supernatural world. These perspectives, these crucial intellectual constructs, have been central to traditional Catholics and Protestants from their beginnings.

The verb, pisteuo, relates to action, to behavior, to actually doing something.[52]

Traditional Christians do things. But what do they do? They confess sins, engage in rituals and occasionally do good deeds, often believing they will be rewarded in the supernatural world!

Jesus of Nazareth probably did some of these things since he lived in a remarkably ritualistic religious culture. But from the few snippets of his life that we know about and the many myths about his activities reported in the New Testament, his way of acting, his way of living, his way of interacting with other human beings was remarkably unorthodox.

He loved and helped the aliens, the outcasts, the sick, the helpless and the marginal. He was a social radical living in a rigid hierarchical social system. He advocated social equality. He criticized both religious and political authorities for their endorsement of the societal stratification structures. Most of his social interactions were socially unacceptable behaviors. He was doing significant radical social things.

For this way of living and acting he was executed by the most powerful institutions of his society.

If one accepts Jesus' way of living as the definition of pisteuo, the New Testament takes on a radical social meaning. The followers of Jesus are called to have confidence in the relational qualities expressed in the life of the man, Jesus of Nazareth. It calls us to live with love, joy, peace, long suffering, gentleness, goodness, meekness and temperance.

All these behaviors may be encapsulated in the words "loving behavior." The action of following Jesus of Nazareth engages human beings in the actions of loving all fellow human beings; not just friends. It includes loving even one's enemies.

These are human activities and qualities. This is the nature of positive, redeeming human spirituality. This spirituality has no affinity with or relationship to supernatural spirituality and its intellectual constructs. [53]

In the world view, in the mental constructs, in the belief (faith) system of Paul of Tarsus none of these qualities were possible without the intrusion of the power of the supernatural spirits.

But if this is true, we are in the presence of a profound contradiction. The qualities of the human spirit, the loving way of living, noted above, are the antitheses of the qualities and behavior of the spirits of the supernatural world as these are portrayed and dramatized in practically all the myths underlying the world views dominant in the era and area in which the New Testament was produced.

The Gods, demi-Gods and all other supernatural spirits, without exception, arbitrarily, whimsically, manipulated the humans to which they related. Even the Creator God, the God of the Old Testament, Paul's God and his "Jesus Christ" demonstrate these exploitive characteristics of the supernatural world. They have power, and they use it, to control and terrify human beings; all this for their own purposes.

Faith and Fear

Fear, the English translation of the Old Testament concept, might better be translated "to be terrified." This terror has consequences.

"Behold, the fear of the Lord; that is wisdom." (Job 28:28) (NASB)

"The fear of the Lord is the beginning of knowledge, fools despise wisdom and instruction." (Proverbs 1:7)

Fear produces knowledge. What kind of knowledge? Fear produces wisdom! What kind of wisdom? Is all this preliminary to supernatural spirituality and the knowledge and wisdom of Gnostic doctrine? Are those who reject Gnostic knowledge fools? Apparently so!

It appears in Paul's letter to the Corinthians.

"Therefore, knowing the fear of the Lord, we persuade men..." (II Cor.5:11)

So, in the New Testament, knowing the "terror" of the Lord is a device to persuade men!

Paul and all the people to whom he ministered lived in cultures where the myths presented the spirits of the supernatural world as terrifying powers. People feared the Gods. They served and sacrificed valued things in efforts to appease their God's anger and thus reduce the terror they experienced.

Paul used this device in his ministry. It was a device to persuade people to accept his gospel. It worked for him as it does for evangelical and many orthodox preachers to this day.

Luke, 50 years later, picks up the phrase:

"...walking in the fear of the Lord and the comfort of the Holy Spirit..." (Acts 9:31) (RSV)

148

Dante's "hell" describes this "terror" in graphic terms. It was and has been the intellectual and emotional context for a major portion of Christianity for two millennia. It survives to the present day in orthodox and evangelical Christianity. It is used to recruit humans to churches. There is enough terror in the "terror" doctrine to engage the attention of multitudes who find Paul's faith formula a "salvation" from such a fate.

This is consistent also with the essence of Paul's interest in spirituality and progressive spiritualization in all his work with his churches. The terror of God is a good tool.

> "Therefore, knowing the fear of the Lord, we persuade men..." (II Cor.5:11)

According to Paul's theology, if a human being is to attain supernatural spiritual knowledge one must begin by fearing the powers of the supernatural world.

---

[52] I was a student at Goshen Biblical Seminary in the years 1955-1957. Dr. Howard Charles was Professor of New Testament. He was obviously engaged with these two Greek words and their meaning. As I understood his work the differences are neither subtle nor circular.

[53] Read Appendix A

CHAPTER 25

The Persistence of Gnosticism in Christianity

We must recall that Gnosticism was a multi-faceted religious philosophical system.[54] Some scholars find elements of this world view in ancient Mid-East regions where Zoroastrian philosophy was common.[55] Individuals with a philosophical bent in many cultures developed their own versions. Gnostic ideas were present in the cultures which contributed to the development of Christianity. [56]

As Christianity developed in the first to fourth centuries, Gnostic versions of Christianity emerged. Two distinctive varieties of this religious-philosophical system were wide spread: Monistic Gnosticism and Dualistic Gnosticism. Both were represented in the early Christian church. At their extremes these doctrines were opposed at crucial points.

The one extreme, Monistic Gnosticism, argued there was one reality, the spirit world. From this point of view the ultimate reality Gods were true Gods, good Gods. These Gods were timeless and created nothing. They decreed that any physical creation was flesh and not real, an illusion.

Other spirits had emanated from this God before the beginning of time. These emanations were spirits (Gods). Some of these Gods, the Elohim in defiance of the Monistic God, created time and the physical universe.

Creation was an ultimate threat to the Monistic God's self characterization. Consequently the Monistic God(s) denounced the Creator God(s) as false Gods or bad Gods.

The Creator Gods responded with an equally bitter denunciation of the Monistic Gods.

We must remember that Dualistic Gnosticism argues that the Creator Gods were the true Gods and everything they created was good. From this viewpoint there were two realities; the world of the spirits and the created physical world.

These two extreme doctrines about the nature of reality were present in Western Cultures. These extremes are, of course, ideal types. Ideal types always overlap. This is remarkably evident in the New Testament. Most of the spiritual characteristics of the Monistic Gods were extended to the Dualistic Gods. This version of the Dualistic Gnostic God is the God of the Old Testament, New Testament and the major portion of contemporary Christianity.

In the context of the first to fourth centuries something of an extreme version of Monistic Gnosticism became popular among some thinkers in the Christian Church. The most prominent of these was the Christian theologian Marcion of Sinope. His followers were known as Marcionites.

"Marcionites held that the God of the Hebrew Bible (known to some Gnostics as **Yaltaboth**) was inconsistent, jealous, wrathful and genocidal, and that the material world he created was defective, a place of suffering; the God who made such a world is a bungling or malicious demiurge.

In the God of the Old Testament he saw a being whose character was stern justice, and therefore anger, contentiousness and unmerciful-ness. The law which rules nature and man appeared to him to accord with the characteristics of this God and the kind of law revealed by him, and therefore it seemed credible to him that this

God is the creator and lord of the world κοσμοκράτωρ (English transliteration: kosmokrator /cosmocrator)). As the law which governs the world is inflexible and yet, on the other hand, full of contradictions, just and again brutal, and as the law of the Old Testament exhibits the same features, so the God of creation was, to Marcion, a being who united in himself the whole gradations of attributes from justice to malevolence, from obstinacy to inconsistency."[57]

The Marcion view point became a serious issue during the time in which the books of the New Testament were written. The references to the God of Creation, in the prologue of the Gospel of John for example, was an obvious reaction of Dualistic Gnosticism to the intrusion of Monistic thought in the earliest times of the Christian Church.

The Bible and the developing proto-orthodox Latin Bishops who dominated the Nicene council in 325 CE church were committed to Dualistic Gnostic doctrines. It is these doctrines which appear in the creeds and became the orthodox beliefs of the Catholic and Protestant segments of the Christian religion for two millennia.

As the Christian Church became organized along the lines of Roman institutional patterns, the threat of Monistic Gnosticism seemed enlarged.

Its anti-Creation God doctrines, individualism and fragmentation were exceedingly disruptive to the Roman Bishop's commitment to proto-orthodox doctrine (Dualistic Gnosticism). Their efforts to stabilize the doctrinal dimensions of their belief system and organizational structures were threatened.

Some of the Apostolic Fathers and the Ante-Nicene Fathers, in the second to fourth centuries, denounced the Monistic

Gnostic Christians as heretics and violently persecuted them. These heresy-hunting bishops were finally successful in forcing Monistic Gnostic writings underground and destroying many church communities.

These Ante-Nicene church fathers promoted Dualistic Gnostic ideas. They were convinced they alone had the truth about the supernatural spiritual world. They claimed to know the nature of the spirits of that world, the character of the supreme God and his interaction with human beings in the physical universe.

In the efforts to stabilize their organization, the formalization of ultimate truth in creedal forms was accomplished. These creeds were the culminating definitive response to Marcion and some extreme Monistic Gnostic elements in the early church.

Supernatural spiritual knowledge is strong, if not the dominant emphasis in many of the 27 books selected by the Nicene Council as dependable for catechetical instruction. These Dualistic Gnostic doctrines, crystallized in the form of creeds, required absolute belief. This absolute faith proscribed any doubt, demanded total uniformity and prohibited any individualistic alternatives.

With those measures some degree of uniformity of belief and ritual was attained. Creator God Gnosticism thus became Christian orthodoxy.

However some extreme Monistic Gnostic elements have persisted in many spiritualistic doctrines of Dualistic Gnosticism practiced by individuals, brotherhoods and sisterhoods in segments of catholic and protestant churches throughout the centuries. Any time there are activities related to deeper spiritual knowledge or a closer walk with a supernatural God we are observing contemporary aspects of such Gnostic thought and practice.

Gnosticism and morality

"Evidence in the source texts indicates Gnostic moral behavior as being generally ascetic... is expressed most fluently in their sexual and dietary practice. (en.wikipedia.org/Gnosticism)"

Paul seems to value these kinds of asceticism.

"To the unmarried and the widows I say that it is well for them to remain single as I do. But if they cannot exercise self control, they should marry. For it is better to marry than to be aflame with passion." (I Cor.7:8-10)

Extreme radical Christian Monistic Gnostics might go further:

"Gnostics assert that matter is inherently evil and spirit is good. As a result of this presupposition, Gnostics believe anything done [while] in the body, even the grossest sin, has no meaning because real life exists in the spirit realm only."[58]

---

[54] Wikipedia.org/wiki/Gnosticism (This extensive article explains the general features of Gnosticism with numerous references to the complexity of different variations in this religious-philosophical system of thought. Scholars differ in their understanding of its origins, history, and doctrines.

[55] Ibid-contents 3-History

[56] http://en.wikipedia.org/wiki/Marcionism

[57] Ibid – see foot note 10 in the Marcionism article

[58] http://www.religioustolerance.org/gnostic.htm...Novus Spiritis Cristian Church

CHAPTER 26

A Summary of Spiritualities

Ultimate reality for Pauline Christianity lies in a supernatural world with supernatural spirits. Since all of this is supernatural it is, by definition, beyond observation, description, analysis or proof by any means known to human beings.

However, speculation and imagination enable humans to construct systems of belief in a supernatural world where mentally constructed spirits and deities reside. In our day these spiritual forces are divided into at least two opposing factions.

It is believed that these spiritual powers, on occasion, come to our world and engage in interaction with human beings. The competition, struggle and conflict which these forces experience in the supernatural world is then also expressed in this created world and in the life of human beings with whom they interact.

Religious literature, from many cultures, has described a vast range of such spiritual manifestations. Many of these myths describe Gods, spirits and spiritual powers of various kinds which invade this world, interact with humans and even gain access to the deepest recesses of the human being.

From this view point the human being is a battleground of conflicting supernatural powers. These powers seek to recruit humans as associates in their eternal conflict.

Christianity, in its major representations, believes that human beings initially are influenced, controlled and characterized by the spirits of darkness in its many forms. This condition is defined as sin, even as original sin, and is traced back to either the creative acts of the Gods or ancestral choices. Such realities, it is believed, corrupt humans to this day. In this perspective humans are innately and naturally evil. This condition, it is believed, can be modified only by the intervention of an alternate, ultimately powerful supernatural spirit.

In Christianity this spirit, known as the "Holy Spirit" or the "Holy Ghost," has a confusing amalgamation with such concepts as God, Christ, Jesus Christ, and in an extreme distortion, even with Jesus of Nazareth. From the Christian point of view it is the supernatural spirit mode of these constructs which intrude into the human social world.

These belief systems have tremendous power! They create the cultural context in which millions of people have lived for two millennia.

In contrast to this perspective we must be reminded that Jesus of Nazareth taught and demonstrated the nature of human spirituality. This spirituality is simply the expression and practice of human love, joy, peace, long suffering, gentleness, goodness, meekness and temperance. These are the marks of Jesus' way of living. There is nothing supernatural about this way of living.

In direct contradiction of Jesus of Nazareth much of Christianity has taught and continues to teach that such behaviors are exclusively a product of an incarnated supernatural spirit. They argue that these qualities are impossible without the intrusion of such a spirit. This supernatural spiritual force, it is claimed, can take possession of a human being and thereby instill these qualities. Without this intervention the human is a helpless and hopeless sinner and is doomed to remain under the control of evil and destructive spiritual powers in this world and the next.

It is claimed also that this spirit will free human beings from the consequences of their sin and enable human beings to have a special relationship with the supernatural world, even in their earthly life, and ensure guidance to eternal consort with God forever. People with this belief system claim an intimacy with the supernatural spiritual world and its entities, forces and powers.

These beliefs have several life controlling consequences.

In this belief system, human beings are spiritually helpless, dependent on the unknowable and subject to the arbitrary whims of the supernatural world. However, for some people, this condition is meritorious. It is assumed that dependency inspires faith and this greater faith yields more certainty of acquiring spiritual knowledge. This condition of dependency leads logically to human irresponsibility.

Any thoughtful human being struggles for insight into the personal and social dilemmas encountered in this confusing world. Christians in their mysterious, supernatural spiritual world conceptions are attuned to a particular view of things. They are attuned to an ideology consistent with the dictates of supernatural spirits which they envision. Thus they think that what they believe and what they do correlates exactly with ultimate truth. Their belief system becomes sacred.

In this perspective our social world and our physical world are transient and irrelevant. This world and its humans have significance only as a domain to be manipulated and controlled by supernatural spiritual powers. Conformity to the whims of these powers is then the purpose of life in this world.

Since the spirit world is, for human beings, a domain of the unknown and the unknowable, it opens the door to theological conceptions and behavioral expressions reaching the unlimited bounds of speculation. The data supporting this contention is evident in the innumerable fragmentations of religion throughout history.

Since total dependency is conditioned on such belief, doubt is unacceptable. To doubt is an affront to the supernatural powers and negates belief and faith which are the very mechanisms of salvation and spirituality. But doubt is a human attribute, a universal human condition. Therefore the supernaturally saved individual must deny their very humanity. Supernatural spirituality requires the saved to live outside of human reality.

These characteristics are the defining features of Pauline Christianity and its derivatives. They are the key to understanding much of contemporary Christianity in both its religious and political manifestations.

Pauline spirituality repudiates the power of the human spirit. It declares the human being and the human spirit to be impotent in the creation of human spiritual beings. It denies the capacity of the human spirit in its communal incarnation to shape and save the human being. It denies the "God in us." It is therefore antithetical to the power of the human spirit. It is anti human in its ideology and effects. It minimizes the human being and denies the human capacity to grow in human spirituality.

Jesus of Nazareth proclaimed the gospel of love, human love.

Some aspects of this chapter are expanded or modified in Appendix A.

CHAPTER 27

A Summary of the Book in Four Dramas

Introduction

This book has been about "knowledge," supernatural spiritual knowledge. Knowledge is the English translation of the Greek word γνῶσις. (Gnosis).

This chapter is a summary of two major Gnostic thought structures: Monistic and Dualistic Gnosticism. These are entangled with other, culturally derived, thought systems in the Bible, particularly in the New Testament and many versions of Christianity.

The Greek word "Gnosis" rather than its English translation "knowledge" is used most frequently by scholars who write about this topic. The Greek word has many shades of meaning which are missed in the English translation. In this book I have been dealing with hidden, esoteric spiritual knowledge. This is knowledge possessed by some Gods. These Gods, according to Gnosticism, have shared this knowledge with certain human beings who have achieved advanced spiritual status according to supernatural criteria.

All human beings are natural physical beings and therefore have no knowledge of the supernatural world. However this has not prevented many of them from developing complex systems of thought about unknown and unknowable supernatural spirits. These speculative systems of thought, these belief systems are the foundations of all religions ever developed.

Whether belief or faith in these doctrines has any relationship to supernatural reality is beyond analysis by any natural human being. However what human beings "believe" is what they "know" about unknowable reality. This knowledge becomes their world view and enables them to center their lives in those kinds of realities. These mental constructs are the realities, the myths, by which people live.

The Bible reflects many dominant elements of a very complex myth sometimes referred to as "The war of the Gods." Human beings, from the beginning of time, have believed in the reality of aspects of this myth. This seems to be the case even in the 21st century.

The core theme of this myth is summarized in an inexplicable statement in the New Testament.

> "For our sake he made him to be sin who knew no sin, so that in him we might become the righteousness of God." (II Corinthians 5:21)

This Pauline doctrine needs explanation. This quotation and its analysis have been the burden of this book and the core of Dualistic Gnosticism in its 21st century version: Christianity.

The following **Myth in Four Dramas**, following is my attempt to summarize four connected, complex plots of myths which have been the subject of this book.

Let me remind you that the singular word "God" and the plural word "Gods" are equal and interchangeable. The grammar might be bad but the reality is correct.

The Activities of Supernatural Spirits
Many Myths in Four Dramas

Drama One: The Spirit World

The Spirit reality

There is an ultimate timeless, eternal reality-a world of spirits. This world is the dwelling place of spirit beings, sometimes these spirits are subsumed as God. This spirit is ultimate, complete, pure, perfect and indefinable. Spirit is beyond description; but is total reality with perfect knowledge and absolute enlightenment. This spirit is all there is; but it is every thing in utter completeness. In all its singularity it is in-exhaustible diversity. These Gods, by self definition, are good. These Gods, in Gnostic thought, we now know is the God of Monistic Gnosticism.

Without explanation, other spirits emerged from this singularly complete and perfect spirit. These emanations are marvelously diverse with multiple characteristics, functional powers and roles. They are actually classes of spirits with descriptive names such as demi-gods, demiurges, eons, advocates, christs, emissaries, Elohim, avatars, etc.

They are all spirits and dwell in the world of the spirits. In some senses they are all Gods. But they are diverse in characteristics and some are limited in power and knowledge.

The total, complete, pure, perfect and indefinable Monistic Gods declared that spirit is the only true reality. Any created physical thing was flesh. Flesh by their definition and decree

is "ignorance of supernatural spirituality." This spiritual
ignorance is the essence of evil.

The cosmic rebellion

A class of emanations, the Elohim. did not take kindly to the
unilateral arbitrary fiat of the Monistic God. They planned a
physical world. By their definition, this material world
would be good and anything in it would be good. This was a
direct affront to the Monistic God.

The Elohim plan actually consisted of two additional plans.
The first of these required the crucifixion of God's Son.
Those who believed and were thereby saved, would
constitute the "Church."

This was the spiritual tool necessary to prove that the Creator
Gods had done the right thing (were righteous) in creating
the physical world. Church participants would become
candidates for spiritualization. This process would transform
them into supernatural spirits and prepare them for
participation in the activities of the Gods and eternal
association with the Gods in the heavens.

These plans were finalized by the Elohim in eternity before
time or creation. Their plans, when executed, would
demonstrate that flesh was not inherently evil.

It would prove the Elohim to be right (righteous) and the
Monistic God to be wrong. (unrighteous) It would prove that
the Elohim were more powerful than the single minded pure
spirit God. It would prove that human beings could become
involved in the dynamics of the supernatural spiritual world
and could even become warriors for the Elohim Gods as they
battled against the Monistic Gods and their arbitrary,
unilateral decrees.

Drama Two: Two Realties

The creation

The Elohim created both time and the physical universe.

> "In the beginning God created the heavens and the earth."(Genesis 1:1 RSV)

There were now two realities; spiritual and physical reality.

With this creation the Elohim were appropriately renamed the Creator Gods. They also became known as The Dualistic Gods since they were now Gods of the spirit world and also Gods of the physical universe. These Gods became the God of the cultures which produced the Bible and the Christian religion.

The Monistic Gods were enraged at this violation of pure spiritual reality. They, by decree, made all physical creation to be flesh. This was ignorance of supernatural spiritual knowledge. This condition produced "evil" and degeneration. The Monistic Gods characterized the Creator Gods as false Gods, bad Gods and evil Gods.

The Elohim responded in kind and labeled the pure spirit, ultimate reality, Monistic Gods as false Gods, bad gods and evil Gods.

The schism in the spirit world was sharp, bitter and irrevocable.

At the center of the created universe, the earth, the Creator Gods continued their work. Their last and crowning creation was a human being formed from the dust of the earth. These beings were flesh and had a human spirit not a supernatural spirit. They had no knowledge of the supernatural world. However they were, in some incomprehensible way, made in the image of God. They could also create flesh things. All this was done according to the Elohim's plan which had been designed before the beginning of time.

On the seventh day the Creator God rested, surveyed his handy work and decreed himself to be the true God and all his creation to be good.

But the Monistic God had decreed that all physical creation was flesh. Human beings would know nothing of supernatural spiritual reality and were consequentially evil. The Creator God did not undo that decree and simply declare his creation to be good.

Which God is right about creation? Which God is right? (righteous) Which God is wrong? (unrighteous) This is the ultimate question of the universe! This is the question the Bible was designed to answers.

The Monistic pure spirit conquest of creation

The Creator God took extended his residence to his own creation, particularly in the stars of the heavens. But immediately had neighbors.

The Monistic pure spirit Gods with their minions (many other classes of emanations), as is the nature of spirit, occupied the Creator Gods' universe; the heavens. This was inevitable since it is the necessary quality of spirit to be everywhere at once and in a timeless way.

Immediately these spirits began to exercise some influence and even control over the physical universe and its humans.

Was this a victory for the Monistic God in the first skirmish in the first battle of the endless War of the Gods?

But the Creator God, being an all knowing spirit, knew this event was inevitable. It was even required for the accomplishment of his ultimate plans!

The Garden of Eden

In spite of what appeared to be a defeat in the first battle, the Creator God still had his crowning creation in the Garden of Eden. They were unique creations. They could choose to obey him or not. He had forbidden them to eat certain fruit of the garden and decreed death and horrendous punishment if they disobeyed.

The Garden was a marvelous place and their life of ease was remarkable. They obeyed their Creator and he walked with them in the cool of the evening.

But the Creator God had made them with a crucial limitation. He had created them so they were flesh and had no knowledge of supernatural spiritual reality.

Among the spirits associated with the Monistic God were devious types of spirits who knew of this human limitation. They informed the human beings of a way to overcome this deficiency and give them access to supernatural spiritual knowledge. All they had to do was eat the forbidden fruit. Adam and Eve did this. The promise was hollow and their disobedience of the decree of the Creator God had disastrous consequences.

They received "knowledge," but it was knowledge of thorns, thistles, labor and the lost life of luxury in the garden. They also knew that the spark of spirituality, the shadow of God, with which they had been endowed, was of no help. They were evil. It was a condition which all descendants inherited.

Their disobedience angered their Creator. He expelled them from the garden, condemned them to death and no longer fellowshipped with them. His relationship with them for ages of time was wrathful.

Had the Monistic God proven again that creation was a bad idea? Had the creation of human beings been a mistake? To admit such a thing would prove the Monistic God to be righteous.

It appears that the Creator God had lost a second battle.

Or was this, in some way, a ruse, a part of the Elohim plan which had been designed before the world began?

A second chance: Noah

The Creator God found one man among the human race who had the qualities for a new beginning. The rest of humanity was a failure and expendable.

The flood eliminated the failures. A new age emerged and a new order of humanity appeared. But within one generation all the old characteristics reappeared. The nature of creation and its flesh had not changed.

Could the Creator God not recognize that his crowning creation had been a mistake? Should he surrender to the Monistic Gods' decree?

The "righteousness" of the Creator God was at stake again in the new age.

Knowledge and alienation at Babel

The free choice human beings did not give up their ungodly lust for knowledge of supernatural spiritual realities and its Gods. They built a tower ascending to the edge of the heavens. As they were about to scrutinize the spirit world the Creator God discovered their willful and disobedient action and punished them again.

He confused their languages. In this social schism he made it impossible for them to communicate. In this anti-social condition they lost the capacity to cooperate. They became utterly selfish, competitive and hostile in all their interactions.

From the view point of the Creator God the "free choice human beings" were a problem, even a failure. Was it possible that creation was a mistake? Was it possible that the Monistic God's decree about flesh being evil might be right?

But the Creator God had declared his creation to be good. Things were confused in both the supernatural world and the created world. Which God was really right?

The Creator God gave up on most of the human race and abandoned them. But he still needed to prove that he was right (righteous) in creating the physical universe and its human beings. A kind of fourth creation episode might change the outcome.

Abraham and Israel

He made one final attempt to rescue a segment of his human creation and thus prove to his competing spirits, that in spite of all the fleshly things they did, he had done the right thing in creating them. He selected from the whole human race one family; Abraham and his descendents. This family was to be, exclusively, his people.

However, being his people was conditioned again on their free willed choice. They had to choose to worship him exclusively. This was a difficult choice in a world where almost every aspect of daily physical and social life, according to their neighbors and relatives, were controlled by many different Gods of the supernatural world.

The Creator God was aware of these realities. Therefore his strictures were very explicit. "I am the Lord your God," and "you shall have no other Gods before me." To help them in this exclusive way of living he provided comprehensive social barriers.

In addition he provided a way for them to ease their pain of failure when they failed to obey; a system of penance.

Penance and its Purpose

The separation from their creator and its consequences in the experiences of flesh were utterly terrifying to human beings. These agonies were multiplied by the minions of the Gods, who came from the heavens, manipulated human beings with fate and fortune in whimsical and arbitrary ways.

Human beings, who learned to like gifts, assumed that the Gods who troubled them might become friendlier if they received gifts. Elaborate sacrificial and honorific accolades were created to mollify the Gods, win their favors and receive their help. It worked, on occasion!

Even the Creator God, in spite of his displeasure with the choices of his crowning creation, enjoyed, even demanded the honorific services he received but was very ambivalent of this whole system finally denouncing it as useless. The sacrificial system accomplished nothing.

The flesh decree of the Monistic God and the death decree of the Creator God appeared to be permanently in effect.

This fourth attempt failed as miserably as the first three.

Should the Creator God give up and admit that he had made a serious mistake in creation. Or were all these tragic failures of his crowning creation part of the greater plan which had been designed before creation and time began; a plan that would really work.

Drama Three: The Plan of Salvation

The crowning creation in its demonstration of total degeneration seems to be solid evidence that the creation had been a bad idea. But the Creator God did not give up. He would take charge and provide the human race with a remarkably creative choice which would have marvelous rewards and eternal blessings; a positive choice would be easy. In all this he would prove that he was righteous.

Annunciation

The Creator God had many supporters in the spirit world. Some of these appeared in the preceding dramas but were largely ineffective in their assignments. But with this final effort, considerable excitement appeared among his minions. Announcement and directives were given to the principal human actors in the first act of this drama.

Incarnation

Gods interacted on occasion with human beings and produced children who were powerful political, military, economic or religious powers who did heroic things. God-men and even God-women (Goddesses) were social realities in the axial period which initiated the pisces era.[59]

Now the creator God himself took charge of things. With his own Spirit (the Holy Spirit) he impregnated a human woman. The child was therefore a God-man. He was, at the same time, the Creator God's Son; in every sense a supreme and utterly powerful God and therefore, a true God, a good God and incapable of evil.

His mother was a human being and therefore he was flesh. By the decree of the Monistic Gods and the plan of his Creator God, he was "ignorant of supernatural spirituality."

His father, the Creator God, had made him flesh. But by fiat, also made him sinless. How is this possible? Paul explains:

> "For our sake he made him to be sin who knew no sin, so that in him we might become the righteousness of God." (II Corinthians 5:21)

His life

In his short life he did everything human beings do. He did this in the physical and human social life of the peasant villages of Galilee. He experienced the total life of the flesh. But he loved his fellow human beings.

Crucifixion

Jesus Christ was spirit and could not sin. He had lived a sinless human life. But he was flesh. He was human. In view of this reality, death was required by the decree of his Father.

In this experience he acquired significant knowledge of the supernatural spiritual world. He learned that spirits do not care about human beings The Gods did not come to his rescue. Even his Creator God father deserted him.

Hades

In the Greek world view, most common people died and that was the end. But prominent people, who might have some relationship to the spirits of the supernatural world, had a different fate. When they died they went to Hades for an indeterminate time. These experiences of death and a sojourn in Hades were intrinsic aspects of being flesh. God's Son endured even this consequence.

Resurrection

But Gods do not die. They may experience Hades; it was, after all, a significant aspect of the supernatural world. Jesus Christ the son of God was very much a spirit in Hades. From the flesh point of view this was an experience of three days. But what is this to a timeless spiritual being?

In a spiritual body he came back to earth for a short time and miraculously showed himself to a few of the believers.

Ascension

The supernatural spirit, "Jesus Christ," the Son of God was reabsorbed into the pure supernatural spiritual state from which he came.

The point of it all

If humans believe this myth they will be saved. Sin will have lost its power to send human beings to the terrors of damnation and eternal torture.

The choice now is simple and straight forward. There are no onerous conditions, elaborate social routines, no cultural barriers and no struggle with the inclinations of the flesh.

In this plan the "yoke is easy and the burden is light." Just say "yes" to this myth. Just "believe," have "faith." This belief commitment will save the believers. More importantly, these faithful human beings prove the Creator God did the right thing in creation. Flesh was good after all. Jesus Christ through all his experiences in this world proved this point without a doubt.

Some human beings believed!

The Dualistic God by the implementation of his plan of salvation had proven himself to be righteous. All the heavenly spirits could now see that the Creator God had done the right thing. The saved human beings (the Church) had been his tool. The Dualistic God finally won a decisive battle against the Monistic God!

In addition it provided an opportunity for human beings to be spiritualized and participate in the spiritual activities of the supernatural world.

This was the ultimate purpose of all that happened in the first three Dramas.

Drama Four: The plan of spiritualization

The War of the Gods is timeless and endless. The Creator Gods needs support in this war. They are seeking recruits from among those who believe in the salvation plan.

Since the War of the Gods is a conflict of spirits, human recruits must become spirits; supernatural spirits. But how do human beings become supernaturally spiritual and what, finally, is the real purpose

Human spirituality

Human beings are natural. They have human spirits. This topic is explored in appendix A. Human spirituality, it must be repeated, has no relevance and no connection to supernatural spirituality. They are as far apart as this world is from the supernatural world of which we know nothing.

Human supernatural spirituality

Saul; the disciples of Jesus and many followers, into their adulthood, were human beings with human spirits. Some of these people, a number of years later, as a result of myth developments such as the plan of salvation became, in the Gnostic view of things, candidates for Gnostic supernatural spirituality.

Induction into this status occurred in a number of ways. Saved people became supernaturally spiritualized by visions, baptisms, prayers and certain activities of spiritualized people.

In all these cases the foundational power performing this spiritual miracle was, from the Gnostic and Biblical point of view the Holy Spirit. This was God's spirit; the same spirit that impregnated the human woman who bore Jesus. This spirit

174

was now entering selected human beings who had previously been saved. They were, thereby, transformed into supernatural spiritual human beings.

They were beginning to know things about the supernatural world, but not all. The purpose of it all was still hidden, a mystery. A significant segment of esoteric knowledge was missing. But this knowledge was finally revealed to a number of human beings in the first and second centuries CE, notably the Pauls whose writings appear in the New Testament.

The purpose of supernatural spirituality

> "For we are not contending against flesh and blood: but against the principalities, against the powers, against the world rulers of this present darkness; against the spiritual hosts of wickedness in heavenly places." (Ephesians 6:12.)

Supernatural spiritualized human beings are soldiers in the army of the Dualistic Creator God in his War with the Monistic, ultimate reality, pure spirit God. Now these recruits had additional knowledge about the supernatural spiritual world and the crucial activities they were trained to perform.

The Dualistic God by the implementation of his plans of salvation and spiritualization had proven himself to be right in his creation of the physical universe. All the heavenly spirits could now see the Creator God was righteous. The saved and spiritualized human beings are his tools.

The Monistic God was finally shown to be weak, powerless and therefore a false God.

This, from a Gnostic perspective, is the message of the Bible. It is a powerful myth. Belief, faith and fear engage Christians with the supernatural spiritual world.

APPENDIX A

Human Spirituality

It is natural for humans to both love and hate. These emotions, these human spirits and their associated behaviors are observable in human beings as they interact with their fellows. These qualities, these human qualities, and their consequences are common to all human beings. They are the essential elements of all human experience and are the stuff of dramas, and novels. They make or break the human being.

The spirit which humans feel in emotions and exhibit in actions is remarkably powerful. The spirit we practice contributes, at every moment, to the reformation or deformation of those with whom we interact; and ourselves as well.

Let us look at the three fold foundational characteristics f human beings: the physical organism, the human social being and the human social spiritual being.

The physical organism

The fetal organism is nurtured in a physical womb where it receives the genetic materials and the nutrients necessary for its physical formation. Its complex structures are dictated by chemical characteristics provided by its progenitors.

The human organism shares a vast majority of its design and these processes with other primates. The few differences justify a classification which, conventionally, we designate as human.

There is also some evidence that, under certain conditions aspects of the genetic structures may even determine certain social characteristics. For example, the fetal alcohol syndrome developed in-utero is an obvious result of the mother's social experience.

There is no doubt that other genetic chemical variations at the fetal stage predispose the physical organism after its birth to express behaviors consistent with these chemically induced tendencies.

The fetus matures and a child is extrude from a physical womb into a social womb where it begins to express the natural consequences of the above mentioned variables and begins to develop social dimensions.

The social womb

The social womb is the primary group, extended family, community and ultimately the larger social group all of which contribute to the individual's sense of identity.

The physical processes continue into maturity and adult hood. They are dependent on a complex of social interactions for as long as life lasts.

It is in this context that the physical human being becomes a social human being and a social spiritual human being. In a large measure they come with the community which the parents provide. These two phenomena occur in the same general context and are in many ways complementary and mutually interdependent. However it may, for analytical purposes, be useful to view them as separate developments.

Through social interaction with significant others in infancy, childhood and teenage years, the individual gradually learns the cultural mores of it's "significant others." A sense of community identification emerges and a self identity is constructed. Through all these processes the individual is becoming a human social being.

Two qualifications must be observed. This is an on going and endless process. Reinforcements of self identity are crucial to a sense of integrity throughout life. In case of a radical change in the character of the "significant other" produced by mobility or other factors the extremely difficult reconstruction of a new identity may be experienced.

As individuals interact with others they soon discover emotions and feelings which range across the "love-hate" continuum. They also learn behavior patterns associated with these emotions.

The social product

In spite of some evidences pointing to the influence of chemical genetic variables in personality formation a large portion of social and spiritual development is a social product.

The human organism is surrounded in the normal course of things by a social group: parents, siblings, extended family, friends and community who have a vast array of cultural characteristics. As the human organism learns, absorbs, internalizes and practices the cultural behaviors and values of its social group it becomes a social entity. It is only then a social human being. It is the social matrix, the social womb which produces a social human being.

The process is never complete. It is an ongoing and ever changing reality. We must be able to confess our incompleteness and open ourselves to the possibility of social change, maybe even social transformation.

We are here in the presence of the social realities which give rise to spiritual realities.

Natural human spiritual development although interdependent with natural social development must be understood as an additional but complementary development.

In essence it is the quality of relationships which is learned at the emotional and behavioral level. Only when the human social being develops the ability to relate in either a loving or hating way are they progressively evolving into a natural social spiritual being.

If the physical human being during the years of socialization experiences loving care, social bonding will occur. Such an individual will develop the characteristics which are constructive for the individual and society. We may describe such a person as a wholesome, fully developed human social spiritual being. This human spiritual being as it matures is capable of nurturing, shaping and creating positive, creative fellow human beings.

This loving interaction of human with human is the ongoing creative milieu which enables humans to create and recreate one another. This is a spiritual power; sometimes defined as "God within us." This is a natural human spirit. It is the only constructive, creative spiritual reality we will ever encounter in our human existence.

There is nothing mysterious or supernatural about this process. The creation of the spiritual being goes on through childhood, into adulthood and throughout life. The task is never finished. A loving human spirit is the only power which can turn a human organism into a human socially positive spiritual being.

Conversely, when the social environment, the social womb, is characterized by hate expressed in harshness, aggression, competition, violence, pride, conflict, humiliation, etc. the developing social being will learn these destructive social spiritual attitudes and behaviors.

The product of this destructive quality of spirit is also a natural human social spiritual being. But such a social spiritual being is a tragedy to itself and every one in its social context. Such a spiritual being experiences the terrifying consequences of social alienation, personal degeneration and a decline in the capacity to relate in positive ways. We may describe such a person as a deformed social spiritual being.

But even such a deformed human social spiritual being may be transformed. It is the power of human love, in its multiple forms of expression, which enables the reformation, even the reconstitution of older human beings who have suffered the deformation, degeneration and crippling that comes from rejection, and the failure of community and its members to do their creative work.

It must be observed that the physical organism has an innate tendency to survive. Some observers of this phenomenon have assumed that this is demonstrated by individualistic, defensive, hostile and violent interaction. Scientists, such as W.O Wilson find evidence that survival, in the long run, is best served by the support of the nurturing community; a social situation in which all in the community prosper as a consequence of co-operation. Some scientific evidence strongly supports the contention that following the way of love is the superior way of living.[60]

I am writing his in a culture in which Jesus of Nazareth is constantly referenced even though the culture, in large measure, rejects his teaching and way of life. Is it possible there can be a new awareness of his life and work?

Many people who would identify them selves as "followers of Jesus" would also recognize that other human beings through out history have practiced the same way of living. Jesus would have agreed. Jesus remains for spiritually creative people in our culture, a marvelous exemplar of a "way of living" that redeems human beings.

Jesus was not a Christian. The 'followers of Jesus" were not and are not Christians. Christianity is a religion which grew out of the hallucinations of Saul of Tarsus more than a decade after Jesus was crucified.

"Jesus' way of living" is a human way of living. It is a commitment to and the practice of creative loving interaction with all other human beings and the very earth itself. This kind of spirituality is characterized by compassion, humility, forgiveness, creative inclusion and social equality. These are real down to earth observable human behaviors. There is nothing supernatural or magical about this kind of life.

In the New Testament these creative human spiritual characteristics are defined as love, joy, peace, long suffering, gentleness, goodness, meekness and temperance.[61] These are not just words or "beliefs;" they are behaviors, they are actions. They are the mechanisms which gradually transform human organisms into social spiritual human beings. They are the essential ingredients in family and community which enable an infant to become a social human being and finally, at maturity, a social spiritual human being with the qualities required to be a contributing member of a stable community.

Jesus way of life calls us to such a community. It calls us out of the agony of individualistically oriented supernatural spirituality. It frees us from the supernatural spirits and Gods that seek to make us pawns in their supernatural spiritual warfare.

We are called to grow toward his kind of human spirituality. This is the real human task. We dare not be diverted by the manipulations of supernatural spirits.[62]

The evolution toward maturity then is a three fold process. Each of these three stages requires the interaction with a primary group who interact with physical support, socialization in the "loving way of living" and a quality of spiritual interaction which enables human beings to grow toward the loving life which Jesus of Nazareth promoted.

It is surely time to escape from the intrigues of the Gnostic supernatural world. It is time to join the human race and begin his way of living!

Jesus' Gospel[63] is interested in transforming human organisms into human social beings and finally into human social spiritual beings. This human social spiritual being has the capability, in the context of relationships, to transform the self and fellow human beings. In this kind of relationship the human potential can be realized to its fullest.

Paul's Gospel, which produced Christianity with all its variations and derivatives, is designed to save human beings from the consequences of their sin and transform them into supernatural spiritual beings destined to live in some supernatural world with supernatural deities and spirits. All of this depends on the infusion of the Holy Spirit."[64]

Obviously these are radically different types of spirituality. How are these different kinds of spiritualities experienced in relationships of every day human life? What are there consequences for individuals and society?

---

[60] W.O. Wilson – Socio-biology: A New Synthesis;1975
            - On Human Nature; 1978
[61]Galatians 5:22
[62] Snider, Howard M. - <u>Jesus or Christ</u>; Infinity Press 2007
[63]   - <u>The Cultural Creation of Christianity</u>; 2005
[64] Ibid – See pages 74-75 for a description of the difference between Jesus Christianity and Constantinian Christianity

APPENDIX B

The Cultural Context of New Testament Literature

The academic study of the institution of religion, has classified three components: beliefs, rituals and community.

Religions vary in the emphasis placed on each of these dimensions. In a general way tribal religions emphasize rituals; correct practices. Religions of the Book tend to stress belief; an intellectual commitment to doctrines. Community religions and their quasi secular cooperative derivatives find constructive social interaction and communal responsibility to be paramount concerns.

In general these components in theistic religions claim to have some supernatural or ultimate significance. They would claim some connection to a domain beyond the natural world and human sensory perceptions. This supernatural experience is the essence of such religions and is associated with ideas of spiritualization.

Religions vary from culture to culture in respect to specific aspects of the dimensions mentioned above. The materials in the New Testament were written in the context of at least four overlapping thought systems. A brief description of these world views follows.

Jewish religion

Saul grew to maturity in the Jewish Diaspora community in the city of Tarsus located close to the North East corner of The Mediterranean Sea.

His synagogue had the Old Testament, numerous other materials and commentaries about his Hebrew ancestor's conceptions of social and supernatural truth. These had been formulated, according to Jewish tradition in the cultures of Persia, Mesopotamia, Chaldea, Egypt, Midiannite tribal groups and the land of Canaan. The amalgamation of aspects of these cultures were part of his Jewish heritage, part of his world view.

But there were other major factors contributing to his world view as he matured.

Roman Mithraism

The dominant Greco-Roman culture of the city of Tarsus and its hinterland had two distinct religious-philosophical traditions. One was a Roman version of the two thousand year old myth of Mithra.

Mithra was the son of a God and a human woman. He was born in a cave, heralded by angels and received gifts brought by wise men. This event occurred at the time of the celestial transition from the zodiacal era of the bull to the era of the ram.

Mithra in manhood, according to the myth, slaughtered the bull and its blood fell to the ground where it produced vegetation and all kinds of new life. Its meaning was clear; the old had passed away and the new had emerged. This transition was memorialized in many rituals.

Greek military forces in their forays into Persia in the fourth century BCE encountered and adopted this religious-philosophical system. As Roman power gradually displaced Greek power in the second and first centuries BCE it was adopted by the military, political and economic elites of the Roman Empire.

An elaborate ritual system was vital to its survival. Devotees meet periodically in caves or catacombs. The scene of Mithra slaughtering the bull was carved in stone and was the focus of the assembly. A mixture of bull's blood and herbs was the commemorative toast in communal rituals. On special occasions a pit was dug and covered with logs. Devotees who wished to be cleansed of the old habits and make a transition to a renewed life went into the pit. A bull was driven onto the logs and slaughtered. Blood ran down onto the heads and upturned faces of those who desired purification and rejuvenation.

Saul, a Roman citizen and a resident of the intellectually progressive city of Tarsus could not have escaped the fundamental implications of this world view. The letters to the churches he formed, reflect crucial features and implications of this religious-philosophical "communion" system and its practices.

Greek mythology

A third religious-philosophical system was wide spread in the Roman Empire in the first Century. It is best represented by the masses of common people, the slaves, the laborers in the cities, the peasants of the rural villages and the serfs on the estates of the wealthy land owners.

This world view consisted of a multitude of Greek myths. Many of these stories had been collected and written by Homer in the eighth century BC. The Roman author Virgil in late first century BCE produced a Latin version of the myths. His work was essentially a Romanizing of the names of the characters, the location of events and accommodations to the ethos of Roman culture. Thus the masses of common people whether they were of Greek or Roman ancestry shared the same myths.

These myths reported the activities of the multiplicity of Gods, demigods, and a host of other spiritual entities. All of these were supernatural in some sense of the word. They could be resident in the supernatural world or come to our world where they engaged in controlling relationships with human beings. The supreme Gods sent their representatives, advocates, messengers, christs, emissaries, avatars and etc., to do their biddings and engage human beings in all kinds of ways.

These supernatural beings, in arbitrary and whimsical ways, manipulated the life and fate of human beings. Consequently human beings lived in uncertainty and fear, never knowing what was going to happen.

But there were, in all these cultures, systems of activities by which human beings attempted to persuade the Gods to treat them kindly. Worship and sacrifices were primary. Words of adoration, songs, and sacrificial gifts of things they themselves needed. In extreme cases the sacrifice of children or members of the community were techniques to ward off community disaster.

Saul of Tarsus grew to maturity surrounded on all sides by these religious-philosophical myths which were central to the world views of his Greco-Roman neighbors and acquaintances. There is no way he could have escaped the influences of these myths. He obviously accomplished something of an amalgamation of this diversity. All these elements contributed to his world view and his self understanding.

Saul, in his Jewish religion, was expecting a saving messenger from the supernatural world, the Jewish messiah. He became aware of the "followers of Jesus of Nazareth" who were promoting a set of doctrines which called into question the authority of his religious leaders and many of its doctrines to which he was committed.

He spent some years persecuting the followers of Jesus and then had a "vision" resulting in a total reformation of his "world view." He concluded that "Jesus of Nazareth" was the Messiah. But in his identification with Greek culture and mythology, he recognized him to be a "christ;" A supernatural spiritual messenger to the whole world.

This christ was more than an ordinary messenger. As his theology developed his "Jesus Christ" was a son of the Creator God sent to do a special mission in this world. This mission was to save the world from sin, more exactly from the consequences of their sin, and ultimately turn them into spiritual beings in heaven.

But there was a way to speed up the process. There was a way for human beings to become spiritual beings while still living in this world. One aspect of his Greco-Roman culture provided the religious-philosophical system of thought to accomplish this marvelous transformation.

Gnosticism

This system of thought, common among the intellectual elites of many cultures, was known as Gnosticism. It was a search for supernatural spiritual knowledge.

The Greek word "gnosis" is "knowledge" in its English translation. In its religious-philosophical context it refers to esoteric knowledge, a supernatural spiritual knowledge. Such knowledge is possessed only by supernatural spirits.

However under special circumstances this knowledge may be revealed to human beings by the Gods or their messengers. Human beings, in these encounters may be spiritualized. They are invested with the spirit of the supernatural world and are thereby empowered to do miracles and even, in advanced levels may have power to cause the supernatural spirit to enter other human beings.

Paul and other writers of the New Testament seem obsessed with the process of spiritualization and its linkage with the power to do miracles. It is difficult to avoid the conclusion that Gnosticism was a crucial component of their world view.

There was an additional purpose, probably the crucial purpose, for the spiritualization of human beings. They were training to be warriors for the Creator Gods in their war against the Monistic Gods. Success in this activity is rewarded with eternal life in the heavens with the Gods. This became a major part of Paul's world view, his gospel and his ministry.

Paul, as he wrote his letters to the churches struggled to synthesize and amalgamate these diverse systems of thought. Did he succeed? The diversity and confusions of 21st century Christianity should invite Christians to raise this question.

APPENDIX C

Myth and Culture

Jesus of Nazareth was recognized as a remarkable man by those who followed him most closely. He was a man worth following. They and their followers developed many stories about Jesus which expanded their conceptions of his connections to the supernatural world.

These intellectual constructs were further spiritualized in the oral stories over time and two generation later, writers such as Mark and Matthew drew on these stories to produce their work. Then the pseudonymous Pauls enlarged the supernatural power of radical Paul's "Jesus Christ".

> "...He raised him from the dead and made him sit at his right hand in the heavenly places, far above all rule and authority and power and dominion...not only in this age but that which is to come. (Ephesians 1:20-21)

Luke, writing in the last decade of the first century CE extended this supernatural spirit and miraculous power back to the conception and birth Myths.

The writer of the New Testament book we call "John" enlarged the spiritual nature and the oral stories about Jesus and makes him into a full blown supernatural God; in fact a God superior to all other Gods.

We must conclude that the progressive spiritualization of Jesus of Nazareth into a fully developed supernatural God was a product of numerous oral story tellers and a number of writers throughout the century after Jesus had been crucified. Later writers continued modifications and embellishments.

These were the early years of our era. It was the time in which the New Testament was produced. It was formed in a time bound culture; the Greco-Roman culture. And this culture was in an axial period. Classical Greek civilization was declining. Rome and its institutional forms were in ascendancy. Ovid and Virgil were rewriting the Greek myths into Roman versions. In this context it was inevitable that the Gospel of Jesus of Nazareth and the Gospel of Saul of Tarsus would be fused and confused with elements of these cultures.

Later the Apostolic fathers, the Ante-Nicene fathers, and even the Post Nicene fathers padded these constructs with their own additions e.g. the trinity.

These events and literary works of the early centuries of our era, particularly the New Testament which is a fourth century version of all of this, are crucial to all that followed and all that we have inherited into the 21st century. They are foundational in our efforts to understand 2000 years of western civilization and its diversities of Christianities. It is the key to understanding the confused Christian culture in which we live today.

APPENDIX D

Polytheism

We live in a polytheistic world. Even the Christian Gods are numerous. Each Christian God one is hostile to other Christian Gods and their respective devotees. Worshippers, in this respect, are like their Gods.

Many Christians believe in the myth of Monotheism. That world view is not supported by any evidence. Let us look at the data that emerges from Biblical materials and anthropological observations.

Abram brought his own God with him from the Ur of the Chaldees. He was an immigrant in Canaan and knew that his God was different from the Gods of his neighbors.

The early Hebrews, their neighbors, and all peoples who were theists were polytheists.

"God (Gods, {Elohim is plural}) created the heaven and the earth" (Genesis 1:1)

The Bible makes reference to many Gods by name. It recognizes that all the neighboring tribal groups who were not descendants of Israel had their own Gods and their own worship systems.

JHWH, the God of Moses father-in-law, acknowledged the reaility of other Gods and gave his devotees strict commandments relevant to this reality.

"You shall have no other Gods before me" (Exodus 20:3, Deuteronomy 5:7 and many more)

What JHWH demanded from his devotees was exclusive worship. The children of Israel were constantly in trouble with JHWH because they often appealed for help to the local Gods of their neighbors.

Most of the cultures of the western world adopted the Creator Gods but at the same time declared their own version of this God to be unique and singularly good. The recent idea of some elements in Christianity that we all have the same God but emphasize particular characteristics of that is a remarkably weak defense of the doctrine of monotheism and is a serious misreading of the Biblical literature.

Just because the Jewish community insists their God is committed to them alone and they believe that they alone are God's people is a blind doctrine. They are worshipping their own God. All the religious communities in the whole world since the beginning of time have been doing the same thing. Every cultural group is convinced their own God is superior and more useful than any other God in the heavens.

Christians alone, among all the religions of the world have a doctrine of Monotheism.

In their self definitions, tribal groups, national groups, etc, view other groups as aliens and often as enemies. Consequently each social group, in reality, has its own God. All these Gods support doctrines which are identical to the doctrines of the humans who worship them. The implications must be obvious.

Christianity since its beginning has been a fragmented religion. In spite of protestations that denominations simply have differing views of a monotheistic God they differ in no essential way from the tribal religions of ancient times.

Witness the national, inter-denominational and intra-denominational definitions of God as they stress their differences. They argue about what their Gods wants them to do, build social walls and engage in conflict and exclusion.

These are like the Gods selected by the cultures of the Old Testament, the New Testament and Christianity. What the Gods want and what the Gods consider moral and ultimately true is always identical to what the religious authorities of their devotees determine to be moral and ultimately true.

APPENDIX E

Two Religious Icons Confused

Jesus was born to a Jewish peasant family of the village of Nazareth about 4 BCE.

The masses of people lived at subsistence levels and were illiterate. They lived under the oppression of the 2% of the population who owned essentially all the resources of the land.[65]

They were burdened with a world view dictated by tradition and a class of religious authorities who perpetuated subservience to traditional myths. In addition they were subject to the Roman political and military institutions.

Jesus as a mature man in his late 20's began circulating in the peasant villages of Galilee; talking about life and ways human beings should relate to one another. This activity became something of a protest movement against the extreme stratification structure and rigid religious traditions of his society.

From the view point of the religious and political authorities he became a serious trouble maker. By the early 30's of the 1st century CE these bitter enemies cooperated in the death sentence for this radical social reformer. He was executed about 30-31 CE at the age of 34 or 35.

From a verifiable historical perspective this is all we know about Jesus of Nazareth.

Jesus apparently had influenced a number of people. After his crucifixion, these people continued to meet together, talked about the ideas of their mentor and persuaded friends and acquaintances to also become followers of Jesus. Jesus of Nazareth gradually became an Iconic personality as the myths developed about his spiritual characteristics.

These followers of Jesus became a threat, particularly to the traditional Jewish religion authorities. This revival of Jesus of Nazareth's gospel resulted in persecution by conservative Jewish traditionalists, notably one by the name of Saul of Tarsus.

Some years later, another iconic figure was born in the traumatic, violence oriented mind of this persecutor.

Paul developed his gospel centered on his conceptualization of the supernaturally spiritualized Jesus Christ. He established churches on this foundation. By the end of the 50s CE he had written seven letters to these churches. Three centuries later the council of Nicene selected these earliest documents as appropriate for catechetical instruction.

If we read these documents with care it seems that Paul knew nothing about Jesus of Nazareth except the crucifixion. But his conceptualized creation "Jesus Christ" became an iconic figure.

Since that time there has been a confusion of these two icons in the Christian religion. In the New Testament the myths surrounding them have been melded into a confusing single myth. In that myth, they are presumed to be the same entity.

In reality Christians for two thousand years, like Paul, have known little or nothing about Jesus of Nazareth; a real human being. And, what is more tragic, Christians in general know even less about Jesus' "Gospel;" a plan for radical change in the fundamental patterns of human relationships and a revolution in the social structures of society.[66]

However Christians for two thousand years have known a great deal about "Jesus Christ;" a mythical "supernatural spiritual being; a product of Saul of Tarsus "vision" and the reformulation of his world view while in the Arabian Desert.

The fused myths have spawned hundreds of associated myths. Many of these appear in the New Testament. These myths have under-girded the Christian religion for two millennia.

---

[65] Snider, Howard M. – The Cultural Creation of Christianity-Infinity Press. West Conshohoken, Pa. 2005

[66] The Sermon on the Mount – (Matthew Ch 5)

APPENDIX F

Jesus Christ, a military icon

"Emperor Constantine, (276-337)[67] succeeded Maximian as Senior Emperor of the Western Roman Empire in 305 CE. Maxentius, the son of Maximian was angered that he had been passed over. He with a segment of his father's army took control of the Eastern Roman Empire in 306 and then attacked military outposts of the West."

Christians because of their many quarrelsome factions and intolerance of other religions had caused social disorder and posed a problem to many Emperors throughout most of the second and third centuries.

When Constantine gained full control of the Western Roman Empire he changed official policy. He was tolerant of religions in general and extended toleration to Christians.

Constantine's army had encountered the armies of Maxentius, through out the early years of his reign and finally, Constantine himself, faced him at the Milvian Bridge entrance to Rome on the 27th of October 312 CE.

The day before the battle Constantine had a vision.

Fourth century historians provide a number of different accounts of this event.

"According to legend, on Oct. 27, the day before the two armies would battle outside of Rome near the Milvian Bridge, Constantine had a vision instructing him to fight in the name of Christ, with his soldiers' shields bearing the symbol of Christ. The symbol was either a cross or the labarum.[68]"

The most important labarum is the imposition of the second letter rho (P) on the first letter chi (X) of the word XPISTOS. (Greek for-Christ)

The Christian author Lactantius, writing several years after the battle, also described the vision.

"Constantine was directed in a dream to cause the heavenly sign to be delineated on the shields of his soldiers, and so to proceed to battle. He did as he had been commanded, and he marked on their shields the letter X, with a perpendicular line drawn through it and turned round thus at the top, being the cipher of Christ. Having this sign (XP), his troops stood to arms."

The chi-roh symbol (XP)

The historian Eusebius, a contemporary and a Constantine apologist, also described the event in <u>Life of Constantine</u>, which he wrote after Constantine's death in 337. According to Eusebius, Constantine saw a vision of a cross rather than the letters of Christ.[69]

Constantine's Vision of the Cross

1524 painting by Raphael[70]

Vatican Museum (detail)

"He saw with his own eyes the trophy of a cross of light in the heavens, above the sun, and bearing the inscription, CONQUER BY THIS. At this sight he himself was struck with amazement, and his whole army also, which followed him on this expedition, and witnessed the miracle,"

Influenced by this vision and subsequent military victory he issued the Edict of Milan in 313 CE.

This edict specifically ordered the toleration of Christians. He also granted funding powers to bishops, allowing them to build churches, restore pilgrimage sites, and spread a unified belief structure.

In spite of this toleration the Christian fractious, socially troublesome behavior continued. In addition they made no progress in developing a unified belief structure.

By 325 CE Constantine became impatient with the social instability caused by Christians. He ordered a conclave of Bishops to meet in the City of Niceae and provided safe passage for any who wished to attend.

Constantine, a pagan, delivered the key note address at this Christian conference.

After months of deliberation this Nicene Council produced two documents which they concluded would produce a unified belief structure.

Contemporary Christians are intimately acquainted with these two documents: One was a statement of faith: the Nicene Creed. The second was a collection of twenty seven documents which had been circulating in various forms in Christian Churches for two centuries: These finally became the Christian New Testament.

Did these efforts produce a unified faith structure?

Constantine was a pagan until his death bed baptism. However he became a saint in some national churches of the Catholic tradition.

Obviously myths vary regarding what symbol appeared in the heavens and what symbol the soldiers put on their shields. But there is no doubt about the effect of these myths on the Christian Church in the following centuries. Jesus Christ became the icon of military power, violence and military prowess.

Other symbols appeared in the following centuries which expanded this core principle of these myths. One of these is particularly significant.

Jesus Christ Conqueror

IC=Jesus
XC=Christ
NIKA=Conqueror

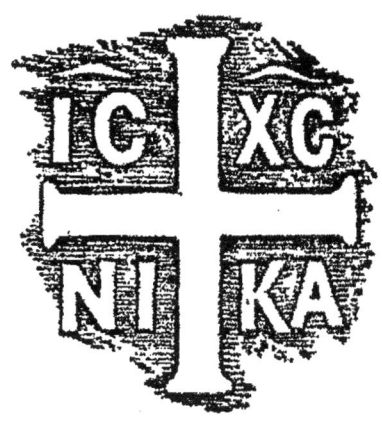

Glossary

Axial period – (see Zodiac below) During the time the sun was moving from one zodiacl house to the next was considered to be a time of transition for all physical creation, particularly human beings. This period of time was known as an axial period. It was the time of reformation. It was a time to discard the old with all its failings and a time of commitment to new beginnings.

There are three axial periods important to the cultures of Biblical times. The first of these was the transition from Taurus (bull) to Ares(ram) which occurred about 2200 BCE. This period generated the religious-philosophical system of Mithraism. The second was the transition from Ares to Pisces (fish). This occurred in the last century BCE. The fish was the symbol of the new Axial Period. It was picked up by the writers of the New Testament and the early church who adopted the zodiacal Pisces axial period and Paul's "Jesus Christ" as symbols of supernatural new beginnings. The third Axial Period will occur around 2150 CE. That will be the time of transition from Pisces to Aquarius. New Age enthusiasts are anticipating this event with hope for renewal of society.

Some historians employ the term, axial period in reference to certain creative periods in history. This may be useful for their purposes but is not related to the axial periods of importance in the Bible.

Bible versions -
NASV (B) - New American Standard Version (Bible). RSV Revised Standard Version; 1953 Edition. KJV – King James Version

God, Gods - These words are interchangeable. They refer to human conceptions of Ultimate Reality. For theistically oriented people it generally refers to supernatural spirits. Although God is grammatically singular it also refers to pluralities e.g. Elohim.

Gnostic - Any one who is convinced they have the truth about what their God wants is by definition a Gnostic. If any one has, or think they have, supernatural spiritual knowledge they are a Gnostic.

He - in this book, is conventional and does not reflect notions of male dominance or patriarchy.

Human spirit – Human dynamic motivations producing human behavioral qualities. These behavioral qualities result in actions toward fellow human beings and all aspects of the natural world. These are human characteristics and not supernatural phenomena. They may be constructive or destructive and every effect in between. The constructive characteristics include love, joy, peace, long suffering, goodness, meekness temperance and etc. These are sometimes subsumed in the word "Love." (See Appendix A)

Flesh - The Creator God imprisoned his Son (Paul's "Jesus Christ") in "flesh." This is the fulcrum term in Gnostic thought. Apart from this concept the word has no meaning in the New Testament. This is the dogma embodied in the term incarnation

Incarnation –see flesh above.

Spirit – Motivational dynamics (principles and/or emotions?) producing behavior and action. In the English translation of the NT the words **spirit or spirituality** occur more than 400 times. In that context they are almost exclusively connected with the supernatural world and its

Gods. The concept is obviously an important theme in Christianity and Gnosticism.

Supernatural Spiritualism – The characteristics transferred to human beings by the Gods of the Supernatural World. They are not related to human spirits.

Supernatural Spiritualization – The processes by which human beings become supernatural spirits. In the New Testament this is a function of the spirit of God. (Holy Spirit) Spiritualized human beings in the New Testament had power to do miracles. Some spiritualized human beings had the power to introduce the Holy Spirit to others who had been saved.

Zodiac - As a consequence of the 26,000 year cycle of the earth's axis wobble our sun appears to make a complete circle of the heavens. In the ancient world this circle was divided into 12 houses. Each house was named by its most prominent constellation. The sun occupies each of the twelve zodiac houses for some 2166 years. The heavenly bodies were understood to be supernatural spirits or the abode of such spirits who had control over events on our earth.

Bibliography

Harpur, Tom – The Pagan Christ, Thomas Allen Publishers; Toronto; 2004

Please consult the extensive Bibliography of Harpur's book. Many authors in his bibliography engaged my attention on this subject over the last 50 years.

Grun, Bernard – The Time Tables of History; Simon and Schuster, New York. Third English Edition 1991

Snider, Howard M. – The Cultural Creation of Christianity, Infinity Publishing; Conshohoken, Pa. 2005
-Jesus or Christ, 2007
-Two Gospels, 2011
The bibliography in the above books are all relevant.

Erhman, - Bart D. – From Jesus to Constantine, The Teaching Company; Chantilly,Va.